# the practical way to healing

# the

HOW TO HEAL

# practical

WITH CHAKRAS,

# way to

AURAS AND HERBS

# healing

JULIAN FLANDERS,
HAMRAZ AHSAN
& ADRIAN WHITE

**SIRIUS**

C.W Leadbeater illustrations courtesy
of the Mary Evans Picture Library.
All other images courtesy of Shutterstock.

**SIRIUS**

This edition published in 2024 by Sirius Publishing, a division of
Arcturus Publishing Limited,
26/27 Bickels Yard, 151–153 Bermondsey Street,
London SE1 3HA

ISBN: 978-1-3988-4447-6
AD012091US

Printed in China

# Contents

# Introduction

Healing can be an amorphous term. It can encompass many ways of achieving well-being. Is it a curative or preventative practice? Are we talking about physical health or spiritual health? And how are the two connected? With 'practical' in the title of this book, we aim to cut through the confusion and build a knowledgebase of how energy works in the human body and how that can be used to strengthen your connection to good health and healing.

The first two parts of the book look at ideas from the Indian subcontinent with a focus on chakras and auras. Then part 3 takes us into the world of herbs and herbalism, primarily from a western perspective. In accessing information about your energy make-up, you can begin the work to get your mind, body, and spirit attuned to the more "earthy" healing that you can gain from herbalism.

All three of the authors featured here are bestselling experts in their respective fields. Julian Flanders has written a number of books on alternative spirituality subjects and his meticulous take on the wide-ranging subject of chakras will permit you to not only learn about the seven chakra system, but will also reveal how you can use the chanting of 'seed' mantras and yoga postures to develop your practice and clear your energy centers.

Hamraz Ahsan turns to the beliefs found in Sufism and the Vedas to deepen your knowledge of another chakra system and also look at spiritual protection so that you can ensure you retain the clear energy you worked on in Part 1.

Finally, you will learn how from Adrian White how to harness the considerable power of herbs and the natural world to create your own remedies. Knowledge of common plants can build an impressive go-to library that can enhance your foraging skills, as well as helping you connect more deeply with the world around you.

As you progress on your journey toward healing yourself and others, you will find a compassionate and knowledgeable ally in the form of this beautifully illustrated book. All three parts can be read as stand alone practical guides or as a whole for a more complete approach.

**As with all alternative therapies, please do seek the advice of your healthcare professional before embarking on any new practice. The information contained here is not meant to replace the advice of a qualified medical practitioner.**

# part 1

# CHAKRAS

# A brief guide

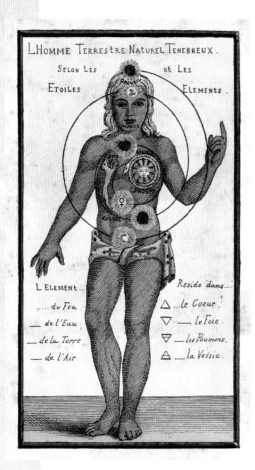

*The chakras according to Johann Georg Gichtel, showing the four elements and where they reside in the body.*

Although they are all originally from the same tantric tradition, there have been five-chakra, six-chakra, seven-, nine-, ten-, twelve-, twenty-one and more chakra systems taught through history. There are major chakras, usually corresponding to parts of the spine, and a multitude of lesser chakras, for example, in your hands, feet, joints and back. But it is the Shakta seven-chakra system that is now commonly accepted in the West. The history of this system goes back to a tenth century text, the *Kubjika-mata-tantra*, which taught a system incorporating six major chakras arranged along the axial channel of the human body, with a seventh point at the top, not then regarded as a chakra.

The popularity of this system was boosted in the early years of the 20th century through the publication of a book called *The Serpent Power*, written by the British orientalist Sir John Woodroffe (also known as Arthur Avalon) in 1918. This was a translation of the *Sat-cakra-nirupana,* a Sanskrit text written in 1577 by Purnananda Yati. This was followed in 1927 by an even more remarkable book, *The Chakras,* by Charles Webster Leadbeater, a prominent clairvoyant and theosophist, in which the author described each of the by-then seven chakras in exquisite detail, including its placement on the body, size, shape, colors and even vibratory pulsations. He also illustrated each 'circle', painting them, as he claims, from detailed accounts of individuals who were able to see the chakras using clairvoyant powers.

Purist critics are often dubious about the provenance of these works, claiming that the chakra concept today bears little resemblance to that originally envisaged in the *Vedas* and *Upanishads* and point out that many of its elements are incorrect and some are even untrue. However, while the seven-chakra system is only one of many models and has many elements that have been added during recent years, meaning that it bears little resemblance to the ancient practices on which it is based, this is the system that has been adopted in the West and more widely across the world. Perhaps even more persuasive is the fact that present-day Indian gurus also use this theory within their system of philosophy and teachings.

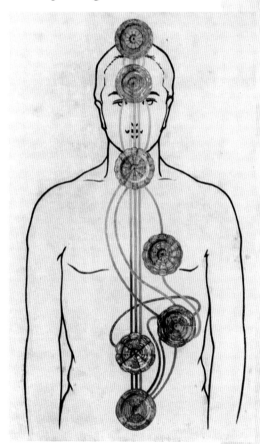

*The positioning of the seven chakras according to Charles Webster Leadbeater.*

According to Christopher Wallis, however, there are certain elements of current Western teaching about chakras that do come from original sources. Chakras are visualized as lotus flowers with a different number of petals in each one. The mystical sounds of the Sanskrit alphabet are associated with the lotus petals of each of the chakras in the system. This is helpful in the meditation used to open each chakra, providing a template for *nyasa* ('placing') by giving you a specific mantric syllable to access a specific chakra by silently, or otherwise, intoning its sound.

Each chakra is also associated with a specific element (earth, water, fire, wind and space), its relevant color, and a specific Hindu deity or deities. The seven chakras are described as being aligned in an ascending column along the major nerve ganglia from the base of the spine to the top of the head. In modern practice, each chakra is associated with a certain color. Chakras are associated with multiple physiological functions, an aspect of consciousness, a classical element, and other distinguishing characteristics. These are all included in the chapters on each chakra that follow later on in the book in order to give you as complete a picture as possible of each chakra.

Below are brief descriptions of the seven chakras and their main characteristics. Before reading, it is important to remember that chakras are not 'things'. As Lar Short, co-author of *The Body of Light*, a seminal book on the inner workings of all spiritual traditions says, 'You cannot cut open a yogi and find chakras, any more than you can dissect an opera singer and find librettos and songs.' But they do exist within the subtle body, exhibiting a strong influence on such things as body shape, health, well-being and wholeness.

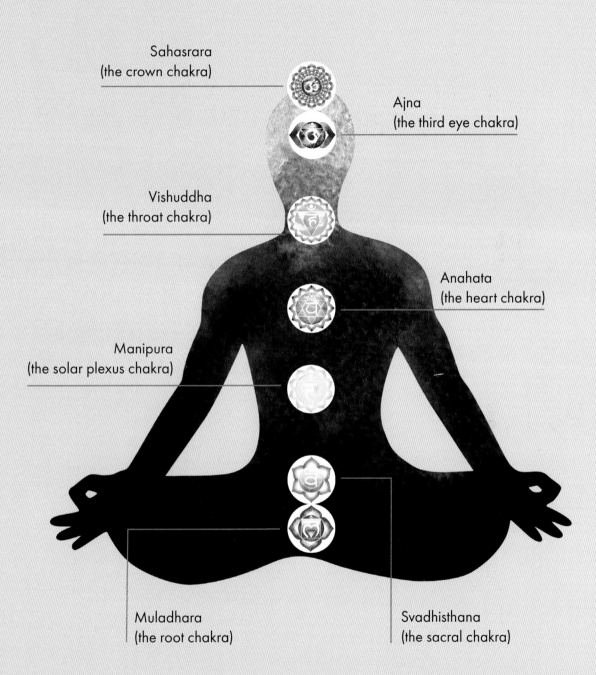

Sahasrara
(the crown chakra)

Ajna
(the third eye chakra)

Vishuddha
(the throat chakra)

Anahata
(the heart chakra)

Manipura
(the solar plexus chakra)

Muladhara
(the root chakra)

Svadhisthana
(the sacral chakra)

### Muladhara (see page 16)

The root chakra, also known as the base chakra, is located at the base of the spine. It helps to keep the energy of the body grounded and connected with earthly energies. Helps movement, survival and self-esteem.

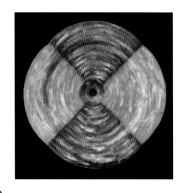

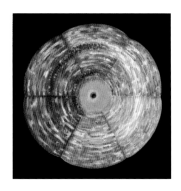

### Svadhisthana (see page 24)

The sacral chakra is located in the lower abdomen, between the navel and the genitals; this chakra is associated with your kidneys, bladder, circulatory system and your reproductive organs and glands. It is concerned with emotion and represents desire, pleasure, sexuality, procreation and creativity.

### Manipura (see page 32)

The solar plexus chakra seeks to achieve balance in self-esteem issues and intuitive skills. This chakra is associated with your digestive system, muscles, pancreas and adrenal glands. Your sensitivity, ambition and ability to achieve are stored here. It can be seen as the seat of your emotional life and is associated with feelings of personal power, laughter, joy and anger.

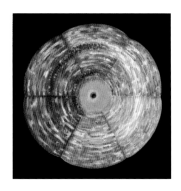

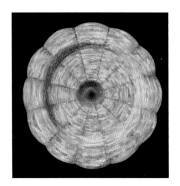

### Anahata (see page 40)

The heart chakra is the centre of love, harmony, compassion and peace. Many call it the 'house of the soul'. It is important to keep this chakra in balance so that we can remain in the right emotional state. Heartbreak or emotional abuse can affect not only the heart, but also your lungs, arms, hands and the thymus gland, which produces T cells to boost the immune system.

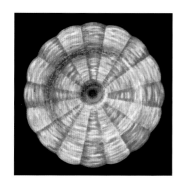

### Vishuddha (see page 48)

The throat chakra is symbolized by the color of the sky, either light blue or turquoise. The name, translated from the original Sanskrit, means 'purification' or 'cleansing'. It affects our ability to communicate. In balance, it helps inspire calmness, assisting us with right speech, honesty and good decision-making. However, not being able to express ourselves properly can lead to anxiety, a cold, a sore throat or an ear infection.

### Ajna (see page 56)

Known as the third eye chakra, this is located in the centre of the head, slightly above the eyes and between the eyebrows. This is the seat of wisdom and insight, and helps keep things in perspective. Its color is a deep, rich indigo and it is said to be the link between the higher and the lower self. This chakra is used to question the spiritual nature of our life. It is the chakra of question, perception and knowing. It is concerned with inner vision, intuition and wisdom. It also holds your dreams for this life and recollections of other lifetimes.

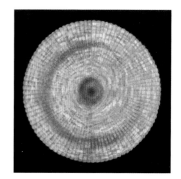

### Sahasrara (see page 64)

This chakra sits on the top of the head. It is the highest form of chakra, which opens up spiritual communication between the body and the universe, the finite and the infinite. It is said to be the chakra of divine purpose and personal destiny. It is concerned with information, understanding, acceptance and bliss. It is the receiver and giver of energy. Some traditions associate it with the color white, others with violet. It is often represented by a thousand-petalled lotus flower.

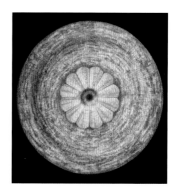

# First Chakra Muladhara

COMMON NAME
**The root chakra**

LOCATION
**The perineum, at the base of the spine between the anus and the genitals**

ELEMENT
**Earth**

COLOR
**Red**

SENSE
**Smell**

BIJA (SEED) MANTRA
**Lam, Om**

YANTRA SYMBOL
**A four-petaled lotus with a square inside and an inverted triangle inside that**

ASSOCIATED DEITIES
**Brahma, Ganesha, Dakini**

GEMS AND STONES
**Ruby, bloodstone, garnet**

Everyone is able to see the beauty of the leaves and flowers of a plant, but few stand in admiration of the roots that lie hidden in the earth below. However, the roots are essential for the survival of any land plant: they anchor it in its place, they absorb water and nutrients from the soil, and they store food. Through this system the plant gains the strength and the power to penetrate the soil, growing upwards towards the sun to produce flowers, fruit and seeds.

The Muladhara – or root chakra – plays a similar role for the human being. Located at the base of the spine, in the place sometimes known as the pelvic floor, this chakra is responsible for your sense of safety and security. As the focal point of our connection to the earth, situated at the top of our legs and the bottom of our bodies, this is the building block on which our existence is based.

This chakra relates to the element earth and provides the grounding you need in your life; this covers basic needs such as food, water and shelter as well as safety, health, material and emotional needs.

The process starts just after conception; at the centre of the soon-to-be foetus is a ball of energy, the *prana* or 'life force', around which the physical body then begins to form.

After birth, the right loving care will mean that the child feels secure in the world, trusting that his or her needs will be met. If that care is not given, or is inconsistent then it might manifest itself as chakra blockages in later life.

# Electrical connections

With stable foundations and our feet firmly planted, we are connected to the earth through gravity. Being grounded in this way gives us the reassurance we need to find our way in the world. With a stable base, we are able to concentrate our energies in a positive way, without fear. Contact with the earth also provides us with energy, as we move through our lives. The Earth is surrounded with an electrostatic field caused by geophysical phenomena, such as ionization, ultraviolet radiation from the sun, convection, precipitation and so on. This resonates with micromotions in the body, such as our heartbeat and the movement of bodily fluids, which is helped by the energy that flows up from the earth, though our bodies, and back down through our legs and feet.

Of course, energy is also generated through exercise, and this is an essential tool in balancing the first chakra. So move, walk, run, jump, swim, play football, get a dog, whatever takes your fancy. Do it regularly, make it part of your daily routine. The more exercise you do, the more energy you will generate.

Being grounded helps us feel complete, balanced and stable both bodily and in the mind. As Muladhara is the first of the bodily chakras, keeping it in balance also creates a solid foundation for the chakras that sit above it.

# Body and mind

The body and the mind are in constant interaction during our lives. It is a complex relationship. The Muladhara chakra is the seat of the unconscious. It is here that we hold our flight-or-fight response. It is here that we store or deepest, darkest memories, our hurts, heartbreaks and disappointments. When this chakra becomes active, it can reveal aspects of our characters that we do not necessarily like, such as destructive rage, deep-seated anger or excessive desires. We can also find that we are suffering from an imbalance in the root chakra, which may be mental, such as anxiety or nightmares, or physical, which may manifest itself as a problem in the colon, with the bladder, with elimination, or with pains in the lower back, legs, or feet. This begs the question as to whether it is better to allow the unconscious to remain buried rather than stir it up and suffer, again.

The answer is not hard to find. It is only by facing the ills of the past can we let go of our fear in the present. Only when we have faced our weaknesses, regrets and bad decisions can we move forward with purpose. We must learn that we are not only responsible for what we do, but also for what we do not do.

Although it hides our secrets, the Muladhara chakra is also the mother who nourishes and raises us. It is also the seat of our dormant wisdom, the stronghold of our emotional strength and other hidden abilities. If you face up to your regrets and the painful feelings in your consciousness, they are brought to the surface where they can be healed. Along with the bad memories come good ones, as we remember how we overcame adversity, how much we loved those we have lost, how we have felt joy, harmony and freedom. You can learn from your mistakes through reflection, become conscious of the right thing to do and find the strength to move forward with the right intentions. In this way, we can remove the yoke of past mistakes and clear our path into the future. Revisiting past disappointments can be a positive process, as it can be a transition, a step in our development.

# The yantra and associated deities

Yantras are geometric devices used to facilitate meditation. The use of these images comes from the Tantric traditions of Indian religions and were made popular in the West by the psychologist Carl Jung (1875–1961) who found that drawing and coloring them helped him overcome rational thought and access his unconscious. Each of the chakras has a yantra associated with it, which typically includes geometric shapes, deities and other symbols. As well as meditation, yantras can be used for protection, good fortune and healing.

The Muladhara yantra, which is red in color, has four lotus petals, inside which is a square. Both are representations of the four points of the compass and four aspects of consciousness: mind, intellect, consciousness and ego. Inside the square are four more symbols: an image of the seed sound (lam – see below), which is said to contain the essence of the chakra; an elephant with seven trunks; a downward-pointing triangle inside which is a crescent moon and a phallus with a snake coiled around it. The elephant, associated with the elephant-headed god Ganesha, represents strength, its seven trunks indicating the power needed to support all seven major chakras. The triangle represents Shakti (female) energy, while the phallus, or Shiva lingam, represents male energy. Wrapped around this is a coiled snake; this represents Kundalini (an energy and goddess associated with higher consciousness) which is rooted in the Muladhara chakra. Other deities associated with the first chakra are Brahma, the creator of the universe, and his consort, the goddess Dakini.

# The bija (seed) mantra

Mantras have been used as an aid to mediation for thousands of years. They can be chanted out loud or silently in order to find an inward focus. When sounded out loud, the sound should be extended so that each repetition runs into the next, creating a drone sound. The most famous, *om*, is the symbol of the Absolute and represents the merging of our physical and spiritual bodies. It is sometimes written as 'aum' because you should begin with the ahh sound in the back of your throat, bringing the sound forward in your mouth to 'ooo' and 'mmm' with your lips closed. This chant can be used to awaken any or all of your chakras, but each chakra has its own seed mantra too. The seed mantra for the Muladhara chakra is *lam* (pronounced 'larm'), the sound of spiritual awakening. It releases tensions, removes blockages and activates its energy. And so the process of awakening the dormant powers within us and raising them into consciousness begins.

# Meditation

Meditation is a good way of awakening your chakras. This will help you in many ways, enabling you to recognize when they are in balance as well as identifying any imbalance or blockages as they occur. The following meditations, one sitting inside and one standing outside, will start the process of awareness for the first chakra. Should you identify a problem, move on to the yoga poses (*asanas*) for help in healing and rebalancing.

1   Sit in a comfortable position, either cross-legged on the floor or in a chair. Sit up tall with your spine straight, shoulders relaxed and your chest open. Rest your hands on your knees or in your lap with the palms facing up. Relax your face, jaw and stomach. Let your tongue rest on the roof of your mouth, just behind the front teeth. Slightly close your eyes.

2   Breathe slowly, smoothly and deeply in and out through your nose. Breathe deep down into the lowest part of your stomach, all the way down to the perineum. Bring your awareness to the first chakra, located between the tip of the tailbone and the bottom of the pubic bone. Notice any sensations here as you take a few slow, deep breaths in and out.

3   Then inhale and engage your pelvic floor by contracting the muscles between the pubic bone and tailbone and drawing the perineum up towards Muladhara. Keep your focus on feeling the pelvic floor and Muladhara as your breath flows in and your muscles contract. Feel your spine lengthen as your feet and legs push down. If comfortable, hold the breath in for a few seconds. Then release your muscles and exhale the air out through the nose. Repeat for 3–5 minutes, working on increasing the contraction of your pelvic floor if comfortable.

4   Return to a slow deep breath with awareness of Muladhara without engaging the pelvic floor. Feel any sensations here as you take a few slow deep breaths in and out, noticing any changes. Breathe deeply into Muladhara for 3–5 minutes.

5   To finish, gently let your eyes blink open, inhale with your palms together in front of your heart, exhale and gently bow. Take a moment or two before moving on with the rest of your day.

# Outdoors meditation

1 Go outside into your garden or the park, you don't need to be in a beautiful place, all you need is enough space to stand and a little privacy. Take your shoes and socks off and find a spot where you can stand on the grass or bare earth.

2 Stand with your feet shoulder-width apart. When you feel your bare feet connect with the earth, allow each of your vertebrae to stack and rest straight and tall. Close your eyes, consciously soften your shoulders down away from your ears and allow your arms to relax by your sides. With your knees slightly bent, bring your awareness into the soles of your feet.

3 You may become aware of a subtle interplay of energy between the earth and your skin. Notice the weight of your legs and feet pressing down on the ground, and feel that equal and opposite upward force holding you in place. Feel strong and solid. Feel the power in your core; feel the balance at the base of your spine.

4 Breathe in and out, smell the earth and the grass and the fresh air.

5 Gradually allow your awareness to travel up along your body, feeling each body part stacking on top of the part below it, supported by your foundation.

6 When you reach the point where your spinal cord meets the base of your skull, imagine the crown of your head being lifted high into the sky, and rest in this equilibrium for a few minutes. Stand tall. Exist.

7 When you are ready, slowly blink your eyes open, take a moment or two, and get on with your day.

# Second Chakra
# Svadhisthana

COMMON NAME
**The sacral chakra**

LOCATION
**The sacrum, in the centre of the body below the navel**

ELEMENT
**Water**

COLOR
**Orange**

SENSE
**Taste**

BIJA (SEED) MANTRA
**Vam, Om**

YANTRA SYMBOL
**A six-petaled lotus flower with a circle inside it**

ASSOCIATED DEITIES
**Indra, Varuna, Vishnu**

GEMS AND STONES
**Carnelian, fire opal, topaz**

The second chakra, Svadhisthana, is located above the pubic bone and below the navel, at the front, and two finger-widths above the coccyx at the back. It sits near the Muladhara chakra, to which it is closely related, both being connected to physical stimuli and interaction. But where memories lie dormant in the first chakra, here in the second they can find expression. While the first chakra is concerned with survival, the second seeks pleasure and enjoyment. If we consider ourselves as vehicles, then the first chakra is the car itself, and the second chakra is the fuel – the passion that fires up the engine so that we can make our dreams come true.

The energy of the sacral chakra allows you to let go ('go with the flow'), to move on, to embrace change and transformation. Translated directly from Sanskrit, Svadhisthana means 'the dwelling place of the self', marking the point when children move on from infancy and begin to develop as individuals. During early teen years, one starts to experience the world through feelings, emotions, pleasure and creativity. For these reasons, the second chakra is often associated with Eric Erikson's second stage of human development.

# Your inner child

This chakra governs the flow of creative life-force within us. As humans, it is part of our nature to create. As children in the second stage of development (8 to 14 years), we create in our play, inventing games and characters, coloring, painting, building Lego models, and so on. As we get a little older and become immersed in the education system, we are generally expected to conform, to follow the rules and fit in with others. This can mean that we lose our creative energy. During adulthood, we get used to doing what's right, follow the latest trends, and stick to what is acceptable. This does not encourage creativity. Indeed, blockages of this chakra are common in adults. While you might be happy to undertake a difficult task that you've done before, if asked to draw a picture or cook a meal without a recipe, you might be forced out of your comfort zone. This is because you have stopped being creative, or stopped taking risks creatively because somewhere along the way someone told you couldn't do it. In order to balance your second chakra energy, you need to take risks and not be afraid of failure.

Play is a great way to do this. A child will spend hours building a Lego tower, a sand-castle or a doll's house. That same child will then smash their masterpiece up and start over from scratch as if it was no big deal. Start to play like a child. If your gourmet meal doesn't turn out right, so what? If your potted plant dies in a week, plant another one. And yes, if your work project is a failure, it doesn't mean your career is over. Channel your inner child and, like the child at play, start again. You have an infinite amount of creative energy within you, so use it.

The second chakra is also the well-spring of other aspects of creativity, the raw creativity and passion that artists draw from. But there is creativity in other things too, such as dancing, singing, cooking and gardening. We do each of these things in our own unique way, and they have a beneficial effect on our physical and spiritual selves.

# Procreation and the joys of life

Of course, many people express their creativity through procreation and the second chakra's association with the reproductive glands and organs – a woman's womb is situated in the same location – expresses this beautifully on a physical level. Its energy is feminine, passive and lunar. Naturally, the sacral chakra also has a strong connection to sexuality, which is yet another way of letting your life-force flow, experiencing life in a sensual way.

The second chakra is also the centre of pleasure, enjoyment and passion. It allows us to experience life deeply and intensively, as the movement of energy flows through us in the form of sensation, emotion and sensuality. This is one of the strongest forces in us, one that can be difficult to tame. Naturally, it is also considered to be at the root of unconscious desires as an overflow of passion that can transform into an addiction or obsession. Finding the middle-point between a joyful flow of passion and healthy restriction is the balance that a properly working second chakra maintains.

The sacral chakra is associated with the sense of taste, influencing our sensual experience of the world – really tasting it. It expresses our authentic desire to interact with life in a joyful way, to participate in the creative dance of divine energy, to really feel, enjoy and taste being alive.

# Balance/imbalance

The second chakra is concerned with our ability to give and receive love. This helps establish a positive identity at the core level of our being, developing a sense of self-worth. It gives us confidence to offer our friendship to others without condition. A person with a balanced second chakra is trustworthy, intuitive and compassionate. They are grounded, open to the world around them, with an emotional stability and a zest for life. In consequence, they are always great company.

As we have seen, the main challenge for the health of your second chakra is social conditioning – we live in a society where, by and large, feelings are not valued, and where passion and emotional reactions are frowned upon. We are taught not to 'lose control' and, over time, can become disconnected from our bodies and our feelings. This chakra is also under threat from cultural attitudes towards sexuality – on the one hand sexuality is magnified and glorified (for example, in advertising) and on the other hand it is repressed and rejected.

Another challenge comes when we lose sight of our inner child, taking on the adult responsibilities of paying the mortgage, bringing up children and looking after ageing parents. During this period of our lives there is little space left for pleasure. We can start losing our sense of play, sensuality and sexuality, and start acting like automatons. As a result, we can suppress our sacral chakra, which becomes underactive. As a consequence we might experience instability, fear of change, sexual dysfunction, depression or addiction.

# The yantra and associated deities

The traditional color associated with the Svadhisthana chakra was vermilion, today it is usually represented as a white lotus with six orange petals. The petals represent six modes of consciousness: *vrittis* (literally 'whirlpools' but here refers to thoughts that swirl through the mind), affection, pitilessness, destructiveness, delusion, disdain and suspicion. Inside the flower there is a circle, representing water, the essence of life.

Symbols in the circle include a silver-colored crescent moon, which points towards the close relationship between the phases of the moon and the fluctuations of the tides and of human emotions. For some, this symbolism also relates to the feminine menstrual cycle that takes a similar number of days as the phases of the moon to complete, although this is not scientifically correct. However, the connection of the sacral chakra with sexual organs and reproduction is represented by a fish-tailed alligator. This mythical creature is said to represent male sexual power; alligator fat was once used to enhance male virility.

In terms of deities, the second chakra is presided over by Vishnu, the all-pervading life-force in the universe; Varuna, god of the cosmic waters and Indra, god of the heavens, thunder and lightning, storms, rivers and war.

## The bija (seed) mantra

The *Upanishads* explain that the five lower chakras are related to the five elements (or *bhutas*) that make up the world: earth (*prithivi*), water (*apas/jala*), fire (*tejas/agni*), air (*vayu*) and ether (*akasha*). Each element has a bija mantra associated with it; when this mantra is sounded it resonates in the chakra and purifies the *nadis* (subtle channels of energy). The *nadis* link the higher spiritual aspects of our being with our mind, emotions and our body. The seed mantra for the Svadhisthana chakra is *vam* (pronounced 'varm', 'vang' or 'fvam'), when spoken it nourishes and purifies bodily fluids and brings alignment with the waters. To create the right noise, start with your upper teeth on your lower lip, and produce a breathy consonant similar to the sound of a car revving, 'fvaarm'. Don't forget that the om chant can be used in healing all the seven main chakras.

# Meditations

The following two meditations will start the process of awareness for the second chakra. Should you identify a problem, move on to the yoga *asanas* for help in healing and rebalancing.

1   Sit in a comfortable meditation pose of your choice. Close your eyes. Breathe gently through both nostrils, with your lips sealed. Imagine you are standing by a shallow lake of still water.

2   Imagine that someone drops a large, shiny pebble into the lake. Watch as the ripples grow outwards and disappear.

3   Allow your breath to become progressively shallower, until it is just coming to the end of your nostrils.

4   As your breath becomes calmer, so will your mind. Make sure your breath doesn't make any ripples on the surface of the lake. As the water grows still again, focus all your attention of seeing the pebble on the bed of the lake.

5   If other thoughts start to arise in your mind, do not try to drive them away. The more you try, the more they will return. Become indifferent to these thoughts, focus only on the pebble. The other thoughts will gradually disperse.

6   When the surface of the lake is completely still, you can see to the bottom clearly. When the surface is agitated by ripples or the wind, this is impossible. The same is true of your mind. When it is still, you will experience inner peace.

7   To finish, gently let your eyes blink open, inhale with the palms of your hands over your lower stomach, then exhale gently. Take a moment or two before getting on with the rest of your day.

* * *

1  Sit or lie in a comfortable position. Ensure that your spine is straight so that energy can flow freely through it.

2  Become aware of your natural breath. How it enters and leaves your body. Where it is in your body. Is it high in your chest? Is it short or long? Don't change it, just observe it.

3  Bring your attention to the location of this chakra, a couple of inches below your belly button.

4  Deepen your breath as you keep your awareness in this area.

5  Visualize a pool of water within your pelvis. A calm and soft body of water. Keep your awareness there as you breathe. Within the body of water is the reflection of a beautiful sunset. The water glows with a beautiful orange hue. Water has the ability to take many forms. From the ocean to the rain, from a flowing river to a deep and still lake. Acknowledge its adaptability. The human body is mostly made from water and is in constant motion (even as you are sitting there in stillness, much is happening on a cellular level) and you are also adaptable.

6  Breathe, be aware of the beauty of the glowing water of the lake. There are no ripples on the water, it is still and the reflection of the sunset is clear. Revel in the scene for a few minutes.

7  To finish, gently let your eyes blink open, inhale with your palms together in front of your lower stomach, then gently exhale.

# Third Chakra Manipura

COMMON NAME
**The solar plexus chakra**

LOCATION
**Between the navel and the bottom of the sternum**

ELEMENT
**Fire**

COLOR
**Yellow**

SENSE
**Sight**

BIJA (SEED) MANTRA
**Ram, Om**

YANTRA SYMBOL
**A 10-petaled lotus flower with a downward pointing triangle inside it**

ASSOCIATED DEITIES
**Agni, Vishnu, Lakini**

GEMS AND STONES
**Topaz, yellow tourmaline**

The third chakra, like the first two, is Earth-based rather than celestial, and deals with what gives us security in our lives. The solar plexus chakra is located above your navel and below your sternum. It functions as the centre of energy associated with ego. It's the source of personal power, self-belief and self-worth. Your solar plexus chakra is activated when you muster the courage to do something that scares you, speak up for yourself or exert your willpower and self-control. You'll notice that in these situations, a balanced third chakra will mean your energy level is high, your posture is tall and commanding, and your voice is firm. However, it's important to note that personal power doesn't mean power over others. It means self-mastery – the ability to master your thoughts and emotions, overcome fear, and take appropriate action in any situation.

The Sanskrit word for the solar plexus is *manipura*, which means 'shining gem' or 'city of jewels'. The chakra contains many of these 'shining gems' in the form of qualities such as clarity, self-confidence, bliss, knowledge, wisdom and the ability to make correct decisions. This chakra is represented as being a vivid golden yellow in color. Like a ray of sunshine, this chakra lights your path and warms your body with the glow of self-confidence. It is here that we feel our 'gut instinct', the feeling that we get when we are sure of the decision we are about to make. This is also where we feel hollow, some call it 'butterflies', when we are about to do something that makes us nervous, like taking an exam or making a speech.

# The explorer

This chakra speaks to your creativity, your personality, your intellect and your ego. According to the ancient traditions, its yellow color comes from the 'solar' power of the sun and its fire. If it is open and in balance, it will empower you with self-respect and confidence. You will be happy, outgoing, ready to face new challenges with confidence. This is the chakra of the charismatic leader, the explorer. A key element in developing balance for this chakra is understanding yourself.

As you explore the third chakra, you are searching for your personal power, what you want to be in relation to the external world. It is here that you develop the 'self', so that your ego no longer needs the input of others to tell you who you are. For this, you must develop your relationship with yourself. The element of this chakra is fire, and should be used to determine your strength of character. It is personal power and strength of will that you can conquer the inertia that comes from fear and move forward through life. The solar plexus chakra can empower you not to be distracted, to follow your true path.

# Criticism and rejection

Self-confidence is a fragile thing and few people can maintain it at all times. Life can sometimes seem full of knocks, put-downs, rejection and disappointments; stress at work or at home can also be debilitating. And it doesn't take much for this chakra to be knocked off balance or even blocked. In fact, criticism and rejection are two of the biggest contributors to a blocked solar plexus chakra. We might start to worry about what others think of us. This can quickly erode self-worth, leading to pessimism and low expectations. A persistent lack of self-confidence can cause people to see themselves as victims, mean that they put up with poor treatment, eroding their resolve to do anything and eventually leading to inertia. Low energy levels, a lack of willpower, and feeling cold emotionally and physically are also indicators of Manipura deficiency.

A closed third chakra can manifest itself as physiological problems too. Due to the location of this chakra in the centre of the body, digestive problems such as indigestion, nausea, ulcers, diabetes, anorexia, celiac disease and liver disease are associated with a blocked solar plexus chakra.

# Getting the balance right

However, balance means that even with self-esteem, calmness and initiative, this chakra also requires respect for others. People with a healthy solar plexus chakra do not boast of their accomplishments – **they let their results speak for themselves.** They are confident but kind. People who have excessive energy flow to the third chakra are usually overly aggressive. They can be dominating, controlling, manipulative and power-hungry. These people are very competitive. **Those with feelings of inadequacy will dramatically overcompensate.** This false show of bravado and self-glorification may be seen as confidence or arrogance, but it is false and crumbles easily. This can lead to serious depression and further over-compensatory behavior. Others are shy and, though they are not prepared to take on a leadership role themselves, are always quick to criticize others. They are also prepared to fail and blame others for their failure.

The key to a healthy solar plexus chakra is finding a balance between being heard without overpowering others with false displays of confidence.

# Feel the fear and do it anyway

The fact is that bad things do happen. The important thing is how we deal with them. Do we sink? Do we carry on in an unhealthy relationship? Do we continue to do a job that doesn't use our skills? Does the fear of ageing, balding, obesity or criticism stop us from living our lives? Or do we swim? Do we move forward? Do we find the courage to take risks? Do we 'feel the fear and do it anyway'? A healthy, balanced third chakra will show us the way forward.

As we have discussed, a lack of self-confidence (perhaps consistent in certain areas of your life or following a traumatic incident or even simply after suffering one of life's regular knock-backs) is a common issue that most of us face regularly. Inertia might be a short-term issue for you. Why not try one or more of the following things to get yourself going? Start slowly and build up:

⋄ Do exercises designed to strengthen your core: crunches, sit-ups, the mountain climber, the plank and leg raises
⋄ Dance
⋄ Practice yoga
⋄ Eat yellow foods such as bananas, corn, grains
⋄ Drink herbal teas
⋄ Wear yellow and introduce yellow accents into your home environment
⋄ Encourage yourself to step out of your comfort zone by changing your daily routine
⋄ Seek out new experiences and unexplored wisdom to expand your repertoire of knowledge and skills

Take chances, take yourself out of your comfort zone. Your natural confidence will begin to re-emerge. It might be a little scary at first, but it focuses us to be in the moment and stop overthinking. Let your actions speak for themselves, and find the courage to act by focusing on your strengths and taking small proactive steps.

# The yantra and associated deities

The use of yantras as an aid to meditation is widespread. They are said to be symbolic representations of divine or cosmic forces, a window into the Absolute. When the mind is concentrated on a single, simple object, it helps clear mental chatter, allowing it to remain empty and silent and to permit contemplation of higher thoughts. The ten shining yellow lotus petals of this yantra correspond to the *vrittis* (whirlpools of thought) of jealousy, spiritual ignorance, thirst, treachery, fear, shame, disgust, foolishness, delusion and sadness, and the ten *pranas*, the vital forces that control and nourish all functions of the human body. They also refer to our ability to manipulate our surroundings, often via the ten fingers on our hands. Inside the circle of petals is a fiery-red downward-pointing triangle, which indicates the spreading of energy, growth and development. Inside the triangle is the symbol of the seed mantra. It also has three T-shaped projections (called *svastikas*) indicating movement. Below the triangle is a ram, a powerful and energetic animal representing the strength and power of who we are in the world. The deities associated with this chakra are Agni, the god of fire; Vishnu, symbolic of human consciousness, and his partner Lakini, who is able to dispel fear and grant boons.

# The bija (seed) mantra

A mantra works in a similar way to a tuning fork. As the tuning fork rings out a note it vibrates and, as we use our vocal cords to make certain sounds, so they too vibrate. These vibrations channel cosmic energy through our bodies, which generate healing powers. The aim of these seed mantras is to help us get onto the frequency that relates to each particular chakra. The seed mantra for the third chakra is *ram*, pronounced 'rang'. The 'r' is produced with the tip of the tongue curling up to the roof of your mouth. When you get the sound right you will feel the mantra resonating from the navel. The sound is said to assist longevity. If you find the mantras useful for you, don't forget that the om chant is an effective healing method for all seven of the main chakras so try using both during your meditation sessions.

# Meditations

1   Choose a quiet place, in the garden or the park. Stand tall, ideally in the sun, and close your eyes.

2   With your arms by your sides, take a few moments to turn your attention inward. When your breathing is steady and unhurried, notice the ground beneath your feet and the space above your head.

3   Breathing in, slowly draw your arms up to the sky; visualize a bright yellow flame igniting in the core of your abdomen. As you exhale, lower your arms in one fluid motion.

4   Continue, feeling the chakra color grow bigger and more vibrant with each inhale. As you connect with the Earth beneath you and the astral world above, feel the perfect balance in which you exist.

5   When the shining yellow light has engulfed your entire body, keep your arms overhead and breathe, embracing a strong sense of your personal power and dosing yourself generously with healthy self-esteem.

6   When you are ready, slowly blink your eyes open. Give yourself a moment and then get on with the rest of your day.

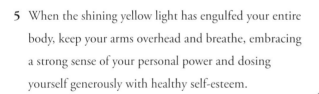

1 Light a candle or a tealight or two if you are indoors and especially if it is dark.

2 Sit down in a comfortable position for meditation.

3 Cup your left hand and make a fist with your right hand, extending your right thumb up. Place your right fist in your left palm, and draw your hands in front of your solar plexus (just below the sternum and above the navel). Close your eyes. Connect to the rise and fall of your breath.

4 Imagine that your right thumb is a flame, flickering at the centre of your being. With each inhale that you take, watch the yellow flame grow a little bit brighter. Imagine a warmth spreading from this area of your body and filling you from the inside out.

5 Now, imagine that you have gathered a little stack of sticks. On each stick, write a word or phrase representing something in your life that is no longer serving you, something that you are in the process of letting go, or need to be. Remember that some things must be let go of hundreds of times before we are free from them. Forgive yourself this process, because letting go is one of the hardest things to do.

6 Now, place each stick into your flame. Watch it catch fire. And burn. And as each stick is completely burned, imagine that a gust of wind travels into your hands and carries the ash away from you, far, far away.

7 Ask yourself: Do I have the energy to do the things I want to do? Do I have the confidence to do the things I want to do? What gets in the way? Often, our energy is drained in one area of our life, and we are left lifeless for the mountain of wonderful, enriching experiences that could be. Breathe.

8 Connect to the rise and fall of your breath. When you are ready, blink your eyes open, take a moment before going back to your day.

# Fourth Chakra
# Anahata

COMMON NAME
**The heart chakra**

LOCATION
**The cardiac plexus, including the heart, lungs and thymus gland**

ELEMENT
**Air**

COLOR
**Green**

SENSE
**Touch**

BIJA (SEED) MANTRA
**Lam, Om**

YANTRA SYMBOL
**A circle of 12 lotus petals, inside which is a six-pointed star**

ASSOCIATED DEITIES
**Rudra, Vayu, Kakini**

GEMS AND STONES
**Emerald, jade, peridot, rose quartz**

The heart sits at the centre of our bodies, it pumps out our life blood, it beats out the rhythm of our lives. It is also the seat of love, the greatest power we have on the Earth. It is through love that we really live, it is through love that we build relationships that make us whole. Without the heart, there is no health, no healing. Without the heart and its love, life is meaningless and we wither and die. Everything begins and ends with love. Love is free, abundant and limitless. Anahata, the central chakra, unifies the physical chakras below and those of the spirit above. As a consequence, it is the most important chakra of all.

The heart chakra is the wheel of energy located at the level of the sternum, or breastbone. It encompasses the heart, lungs, sternum, clavicle, shoulder blades, breast tissue, thymus gland and rib cage. The arms and hands are also extensions of this chakra. The heart is made of a unique type of muscle tissue called cardiac muscle. This allows the heart to beat without getting tired. Cardiac muscle has a higher percentage of mitochondria – the power sources of the cells – than skeletal muscle and so it does not fatigue.

But this tireless service cannot happen unless the heart itself is nourished first. When the oxygen-rich blood leaves the heart it travels through the aorta and out into the body. The first branch off of the aorta is back to the muscles of the heart itself. The first thing the heart does is nourish itself. It serves the entire body every day, for our whole life, but it will always take care of its own needs first.

# Love and judgement

When we think of love, it is easy to be trite: perhaps we think about innocent babies, or puppies or kittens. Perhaps we think of twee images of kids with big eyes or stock phrases like 'love means never having to say you're sorry'. We might also think of steamy sex that we've already had or are looking forward to. But these concepts are not really sustainable over time. Babies and puppies grow, statistically the 'in love' feeling of a romantic relationship lasts about two years and is part of your primeval need to make sure the human race continues.

The heart has more spiritual concerns. Just as it nourishes itself first, so it allows us to love ourselves first, then to love others, to let others love us, and to give and receive love from all of humanity. What the heart really wants is unconditional love and that is a challenge; the challenge to sustain this feeling through the grind of daily life after those initial two years, to love those we judge and to love ourselves. It is only when you have love and compassion for yourself, that you can truly love others in a healthy, happy and healing way.

The heart's message is that you can't really help others unless you help yourself. If we judge and condemn our frailties and our faults, as we do those of others, we will find it hard to love. If a mother dedicates herself wholly to her child and takes no rest or nourishment for herself, then both she and the child will suffer. If a doctor spends too much time with patients and not enough on rest, then mistakes might result. A balanced heart chakra must begin with self-care.

# Compassion and forgiveness

As we journey through the vicissitudes of our emotional lives, we should seek balance. When the heart chakra is balanced it allows us to experience feelings of compassion, selflessness and healing. The world revolves around ourselves and our feelings. Compassion helps us realize that we are not the only ones suffering, it reminds us that we are all in the same boat. This unifies us, connecting us with the whole of humanity. If the heart is too weak, we lack trust and disconnect from others. If it is too open then we can easily be overwhelmed by sympathy for others. Over-attachment can make us desperate for connections, a need for detachment might make us push people away rather than risk being vulnerable. The solution is to recognize our own human-ness, accept our faults and failings as well as those of others, to trust that the need for love and compassion will be met.

In terms of romantic love and friendship, it is impossible to avoid situations where someone might hurt you. When you get hurt, you have several choices. You can live in the place of grievances, unable to forgive. You can hold on to the bad feelings, develop anger, bitterness and resentment. As well as depression, physical afflictions caused by the blockage in the fourth chakra can include cardiac disease, arrhythmia, pneumonia, asthma, allergies and lung conditions. Or you can look that pain in the face, feel it and then let it go. Your mind and your ego might tell you otherwise, but it really is as simple as that.

The Sanskrit name for the heart chakra, Anahata, means 'unhurt', 'unstruck' or 'unbeaten'. Symbolically, this means that beneath the hurts and grievances of past experiences lies a pure and spiritual place where no hurt exists.

# The yantra and associated deities

The anahata yantra features a lotus flower with 12 lustrous green petals, which match the divine qualities of the heart. In the centre are two overlapping, intersecting triangles, making a shape known as a *shatkona* and resembling the Star of David. The six points of the star are said to represent the other six chakras. The triangle facing upwards symbolizes Shiva, the male principle, matter rising to meet spirit. The other triangle, facing downward, symbolizes Shakti, the female principle, as spirit descends to inhabit the body. A balance is attained when these two forces are joined in harmony; this is the source of all creation. Inside the central part of the shatkona is the symbol for the seed mantra *yam*, and a golden triangle indicating the divine light that can be revealed when the chakra is fully opened. Inside that, a crescent moon lights the path to enlightenment and shows the psychic blocks that must be dissolved to achieve it. The chakra's associated animal is the black antelope or gazelle, symbolizing the lightness, speed and freedom of the fourth chakra's element, air. The goddess presiding over this chakra is Kakini, who synchronizes the beat of our hearts with the beat of the cosmos. The presiding deity is Rudra, the manifestation of Shiva, while seed mantra yam (see below) is believed to be the sound form of Vayu, lord of the wind.

# The bija (seed) mantra

The name mantra is taken from the Sanskrit words *man*, meaning 'to think' and *tra*, meaning 'liberate'. The use of mantras for help in meditation was adopted by Hatha yoga practitioners for use in keeping focus during their sessions. They are of particular help in keeping your mind focused on your breath. Chanting a mantra during practice can help to reduce your *chitta vritti*, or mind chatter. The seed mantra for the heart chakra is *yam* (pronounced 'yarm' or 'yang'). Anahata is the centre of the seven main chakras, where the physical body and the spiritual body meet. Therefore it affects both physical and spiritual well-being. The mantra gives control over the breath and is said to promote love, compassion and forgiveness. Always remember that you can prolong your mantra session by chanting om, the most sacred syllable symbol and mantra of Brahman, the Almighty God in Hinduism, creator of all existence.

# Meditations

1   Sit in a comfortable position, either cross-legged on the floor or in a chair. Sit up tall with your spine straight, your shoulders relaxed and your chest open. Hold your palms together and lightly press the knuckles of the thumbs into the sternum at the level of your heart (you should feel a little notch where the knuckles magically fit). Breathe slowly, smoothly and deeply into your stomach and chest. Lightly close your eyes.

2   Let go of any thoughts or distractions and let your mind focus on feeling the breath moving in and out of your body. Once your mind feels quiet and still, bring your focus to the light pressure of the thumbs pressing against your chest and feel the beating of your heart. Keep this focus for a few minutes.

3   Then, gently release your hands and rub the palms together, making them warm and energized. Place your right palm in the centre of your chest and your left hand on top of your right. Close your eyes and feel the centre of your chest warm and radiant, full of energy. See this energy as an emerald green light, radiating out from the centre of your heart into the rest of your body. Feel this energy flowing out into your arms and hands, and flowing back into the heart. Stay with this visualization for a few minutes.

4   When you feel completely soaked with heart chakra energy, gently release your palms and turn them outwards with the elbows bent, the shoulders relaxed and the chest open. Feel or visualize the green light love energy flowing out of your palms and into the world. You can direct it towards specific loved ones in your life or to all sentient beings.

5   To end your meditation, inhale as you push your arms up towards the sky, connecting with the heavens, then exhale and lower the palms lightly to the floor, connecting with the earth. Take a moment or two before moving on with the rest of your day.

1 Sit down in a comfortable position. Soften and then close your eyes and allow your mind to relax. Sit tall with your spine and neck long and your shoulders relaxed. Begin to focus on your breath. As you inhale and exhale, focus on different parts of your body and release any tension you feel there.

2 Let go of your thoughts for a moment, feel yourself deeply relaxed. Then focus your attention on your heart. Think of it as a space and feel the breath enter and leave that space. Feel your heart safe, secure and relaxed.

3 Your heart is a point of awareness, the point where feelings enter. Feel whatever is in there, it might be peace, it might be light, you might feel stress, disappointment or longing. Don't strain to find anything, just feel whatever is in there, allow it to just be.

4 Keeping your attention there, breathe gently, sense the breath flowing through your heart. Visualize a soft, pastel light or coolness pervading the chest. Now imagine that with each nurturing and nourishing breath, you're wiping away any dirt or dust that's covering your heart. Imagine that your breath is actually inhaling into the heart and exhaling out of the heart. Be here, with this breath for several moments.

5 As you breathe, ask your heart if it wants to say something. For the next few minutes, sit and listen for an answer. It may stay silent and at peace, but it may release emotions, memories, fears and dreams long stored inside. This may release strong emotions, a quickness of breath, even tears. Whatever happens, let the experience be what it is. If you drift off to sleep or daydream, don't worry. Just bring back your attention to your heart.

6 When you're ready, open your eyes and bring your hands and palms together at your heart centre. Bow to your heart and tell it you'll be with it again soon. Thank it for its loving wisdom and daily guidance.

# Fifth Chakra Vishuddha

COMMON NAME
**The throat chakra**

LOCATION
**The throat, thyroid, parathyroid, jaw, neck, mouth, tongue and larynx**

ELEMENTS
**Sound/space/ether**

COLOR
**Bright blue**

SENSE
**Hearing**

BIJA (SEED) MANTRA
**Ham, Om**

**Yantra symbol**

**A circle of 16 lotus petals, inside which is a downward pointing triangle**

ASSOCIATED DEITIES
**Ganga, Sarasvati**

GEMS AND STONES
**Sapphire, blue topaz, aquamarine, lapis lazuli**

The fifth chakra, Vishuddha, is the chakra of communication. Human communication in terms of languages, words and sentences is something that distinguishes us from other species. This use of language is a gift, but one that can be used to heal and harm. Having a voice allows us to express ourselves, to our family, to our friends, to everyone. It gives us self-expression, the right to speak and be heard, a voice in the world. It allows to say what is in our heart and soul. It makes us who we are. With communication comes sound, the primary element of this chakra.

The word vishuddha is Sanskrit for 'purification' or 'pure wisdom', and a major challenge of this energy centre is in finding the wisdom to determine how to communicate in ways that do justice to you, to others and to any higher consciousness or higher being. In consequence, this is the first of the three spiritual chakras. It sits at the centre of the neck, and forms the passage between the body and the head. It is said to be the bridge between our hearts and our minds, our bodies and our spirits.

When blocked, this chakra can make you tongue-tied and unable to express your feelings. You may find that your ability to attract what you want is hampered by an inability to use the right words at the right time. When functioning well, you are able to maintain a strong, balanced relationship with those around you and with the higher realms. Mantras are often used in order to ensure that this chakra is operating to the best of its ability.

# Speaking and listening

Communication involves both speaking and listening. The major life forces of this chakra are sound, vibration and resonance. In order to verbalize our ideas, we must pay attention to how we say the words. Your voice is not merely words, but how you say them. Babies and dogs don't understand the words you say, but through the rhythm and resonance of the sound, they will understand the message. Our voices resonate with the sound of the language we use, so if we speak in a clear and inviting way, others will pick up the rhythm, hearing that and hearing what we actually say.

Of course, it's not always that easy. Authentic expression is not something that comes easily. There's a delicate dance between saying what you mean and being tactful. It's often easier to say what you think the other person may want to hear instead of speaking the truth. Fear of not being accepted, or judgment from the other may hinder your truthful verbal expression.

Listening is another aspect of the fifth chakra. The highest form of listening does not mean shutting up and thinking about the next point you are going to make, while pretending to listen when the other person is talking. It means giving the other person your full attention and really hearing what they say. This might even mean putting away your mobile or turning your computer off and waiting to hear the other person completely before responding.

# Telling the truth

Work on the lower chakras will help prepare you for this. When you align the first and second chakras, it helps with overcoming fear. Opening the third chakra helps you to feel your personal power and have the confidence to express yourself. Knowing what's in your heart comes when you align the fourth chakra. Then, when it comes to verbalizing your needs, desires and opinions, you're better able to determine how to be truthful to yourself and others. It is to this process that the word *vishuddha*, 'purifier', refers.

Dr David Simon, a world-renowned authority in the field of mind-body medicine, often quoted the following ancient wisdom. He said that there are three gateways you should cross before speaking:

⬥ First, ask yourself, 'Is what I am about to say true?'
⬥ If so, proceed to the second gateway and ask, 'Is what I am about to say necessary?'
⬥ If the answer is yes, go to the third gateway and ask yourself, 'Is what I am about to say kind?'

Speaking your highest truth doesn't mean you're allowed to be hurtful or critical. The truth from your spiritual essence will come across as kind and compassionate.

# Between the heart and the head

In *The Descent of Man* (1871), Charles Darwin had a theory that human voices developed when chest and throat muscles contracted in excitement or fear, suggesting that voice and emotion come from the same impulse. Might this be why a lump in the throat is often the first sign of emotional distress? When someone feels anxiety or tension, their speaking voice is affected. Of course, the opposite is true. Your mood can be lifted by chanting and through yoga poses, for example, and many people swear by the restorative effects of singing, particularly singing in a choir. Biologists tell us that this is because of breathing, the release of endorphins, and because singing gets more oxygen to the blood.

But there is more to it than that, singing touches something deep inside us. Why is it that all spiritual practices sing hymns or mantras? They are used to clear the mind and help us to unite with a divine entity. Ann Dyer, a yoga instructor and singer, explains: 'The voice lies between the heart and the head. So, on a very basic level, the act of chanting brings together your intellectual awareness with your heart awareness.' This idea is backed up by another singing yogi, Suzanne Sterling, who explains that, 'At the molecular level, we are vibrating entities,' and because the voice is a vibration it communicates directly with our core. When we allow certain tones to run through our bodies, it can bring us back to harmony.

Western medicine is catching on to this idea too and listening to music is recognized as a part of therapy and pain and stress management. Studies carried out during the last thirty years have proved that singing can have both physical and psychological benefits. Ann Dyer recommends yoga and daily chanting. 'The more familiar your voice becomes to you,' she says, 'the more it will begin to reveal your truest self.' Your state of being is reflected in your voice, or as she calls it, 'the barometer of your being'.

A healthy and well-balanced fifth chakra will enable you to express yourself, though your voice, in a manner that is nurturing both for yourself and for others. Those who speak too softly may be unable to speak their truth or may be oppressed in some way. Those who shout are clearly not listening to others, and their conversations are most likely to be rather short. They would do well to take notice of the saying that 'in order to be a great conversationalist, try listening'. There are many symptoms of an unbalanced Vishuddha chakra, including a stiff neck, sore throat, blocked ears, swollen glands and laryngitis.

# Yantra and associated deities

The yantra symbol for Vishuddha is a sixteen-petal lotus around a white circle, thought to represent the full moon or the element ether. On each petal is a letter from the Sanskrit alphabet through which communication is possible. Within this circle is a silver crescent, the symbol of the cosmic sound *nadam* (the 'inner music' that we hear when we stop chanting), indicating purity in the sound of silence. There is also a downward pointing triangle, *akasa mandala*, which represents Shakti, the female power of creation. Inside the triangle is the symbol for the seed mantra *ham*. Below them is the elephant with the seven trunks, Alravata, also present in the Muladhara yantra, who serves all the major chakras with his strength and power. The deity that governs the fifth chakra is Sarasvati, the goddess of flow, speech, knowledge and the arts, while Ganga (named after the river Ganges), symbolizes the purification of sins granted to those who bathe in its waters every day.

# The bija (seed) mantra

Mantras, particularly single syllable bija mantras, are usually chanted for their healing sound vibrations, rather than any specific meaning. They are thought to clear the subtle energy pathways in the body in order to create positive change. Chant the bija mantras, either one at a time or in sequence. Used in sequence with the chakras, they will resonate up and down the spine. The first sound (consonant) should be shorter than the second, and the final sound, usually 'm' or 'n' should be held for longer. Repetition can help you access a meditative state. The bija mantra for the vishuddha chakra is *ham* (pronounced 'hum' or 'hang'). The 'h' sound is produced at the back of the throat. This chant is said to energize the throat and the brain, bringing sweetness and harmony to your voice. If chanting is helpful for you, you can extend the session by using the om chant, which is helpful in opening all of your chakras. The two chants can even be sung together, as in 'aumhum'.

# Meditation

1 Sit down in a comfortable position. Shut your eyes and take a long, deep breath. As you exhale, move your attention to your throat and imagine a sapphire-blue chakra. The blue glow of the chakra spreads like a vibration or a pulse from your throat to fill your neck and head first and then the rest of your body.

2 Imagine walking through a forest on a narrow path that is lined on both sides by huge shade-giving trees. You hear the sounds of insects, of small animals scurrying around and of chirping birds. In the distance, a stream flowing over its rocky bed makes a pleasant gurgling sound.

3 You find a small clearing in which a giant log has fallen on the forest floor. You walk up to it and sit with your back resting against the log.

4 The sounds of the forest become even more evident to you. There is a magical quality to them and you can now hear the faintest of sounds. The whole forest is playing a symphony, especially for you.

5 Now see your fifth chakra spinning and gaining strength. As it spins faster, a blue light washes over you and pervades every cell, every pore in your body.

6 Breathe deeply and feel the energy funnelling into your throat, which is bursting with dazzling blue light. Rest in this awareness.

7 Gently stand up and start walking back from the clearing to the edge of the forest, where you first started. Look back at the singing forest and feel at one with it.

8 When you are ready, open your eyes, stand up and get on with the rest of your day.

# Second throat meditation

1  Sit in a chair with your feet flat on the floor, or on a cushion, wherever you feel comfortable. Slowly blink your eyes closed. Bring your awareness to your breath. Notice the rise and fall of your chest, the natural rhythm of your breathing. Sit and breathe for a few moments.

2  If you find your thoughts wandering, let them. Welcome the thoughts, then gently let them go by coming back to this meditation. Now, make two or three deep yawns. You can 'fake yawn' until a real one comes along. Then bring your attention back to the breath. Notice the natural rhythm of your breathing.

3  At the base of the throat is your throat chakra. Imagine that it is a tiny sky-blue light, spinning. With each breath, grow this blue light. Expand it first to your neck. Then expand again to the mouth, then the ears, then your entire head.

4  Take another breath and continue to expand this light. Expand until it is all around you and you are in a bubble of blue light. Hold that light all around you for three breaths. Focus this beautiful blue light back on the throat. Coat the throat with the light, both inside and out. Illuminate the voice box, the thyroid and all around the neck. Send this light to your mouth to coat your teeth, tongue, and lips. This light expands to your ears, awakening your ability to listen. This light heals all these areas as it moves over them. Breathe in the light.

5  Keep your eyes closed or hooded as you near the end of this meditation. It's important to come out of meditation slowly. Bring your awareness back to the breath. Allow yourself to feel the in and out rhythm of the rise and fall of the breath.

6  On your next inhale, wiggle your fingers and toes. Gently shift your arms or legs as needed.

7  When you're ready, open your eyes with a soft downward gaze. Keep your focus inward. Open your eyes fully when you're ready.

# Sixth Chakra
# Ajna

COMMON NAME
**The brow or third-eye chakra**

LOCATION
**The centre of the head, between and
slightly above the level of the eyebrows**

ELEMENT
**Light**

COLOR
**Deep blue/indigo**

SENSE
**Sight**

BIJA (SEED) MANTRA
**Om**

YANTRA SYMBOL
**Two white lotus petals around a circle,
inside which is a downward-pointing triangle**

ASSOCIATED DEITIES
**Shiva, Hakini Shakti**

GEMS AND STONES
**Diamonds, emeralds, sapphire**

The sixth chakra is located in the area of the third eye, which is found in the space between and slightly above the eyebrows. It encompasses the pituitary gland, the eyes, head and the lower part of the brain. An invisible yet powerful third eye, this is your centre of intuition, often known as the 'seat of the soul'. It is a metaphorical eye, often marked on a Hindu's forehead with a red dot. Ajna, which in Sanskrit means 'beyond wisdom', is a spiritual chakra and, if you let it, it will lead you to an inner knowledge.

A current theme in spiritual teaching is that the world is an illusion, and that you must search through the dogma – from our culture, politics and social structures – to arrive at your own personal truth. But this is easier said than done. After all, we can all see solutions to others' problems more easily than we can see our own. Our left brain also does a great job of hiding inner truth from our consciousness. How often do you find yourself thinking, 'Oh, that can't possibly happen', moments before it does? We have an innate ability to rationalize everything so that we can stay in our comfort zones and continue to believe in our illusions, even though they are often based on fear. Deep inside us all, we hope that there is a better and higher way of being. One without fear of making mistakes or doing wrong and instead filled with joy and happiness. What we must do to find this is take notice of the truths we see through our third eye, the chakra of wisdom and intuition.

# Your 'sixth sense'

Even before birth, a baby starts to experience the world through its physical senses: hearing its mother's heartbeat, listening to muffled sounds, tasting, touching, and even seeing degrees of light. By the time you are born, you have already learned to trust these senses. While they are essential tools for life in the physical world, they are of little use in a person's spiritual life.

While your physical eyes see things through the reflection of light (without light, the physical eye does not see at all), your third eye 'sees' beyond the physical, going into the world of imagination, visualization and clairvoyance. The third eye sees using a different kind of light, the shining light of spiritual insight.

Before the advent of modern technology, intuition was an essential tool. Humans had more reason to rely on their primal instincts and signals from the environment to guide them. Just like birds are said to know when an earthquake is about to occur and cats know when it's time for dinner even though they can't read a clock, so humans have an intuitive 'sixth' sense. We've all heard stories of people having hunches that turn out to be correct, or saying 'I felt that someone was following me', or 'Something about it didn't feel quite right'. More often than not though, we ignore the feeling. This is because we have lost touch with intuition and our ability to trust it.

# Decisions, decisions

Trusting in your inner sense is a huge help in making decisions. This is not a fail-safe method but it means continuing to use your mind, your intellect and your ego, as usual, but adding your soul to the decision-making process. The best help will come from a healthy Ajna chakra. Like all the spiritual chakras, it is best balanced through meditation. Someone with an open and balanced third eye chakra is better able to separate truth from illusion, thereby developing trust in their inner wisdom. Using the mindful skills developed in this emotional centre, allows the person to receive guidance and inspiration from their creativity and intuition. This is emotional intelligence and allows the individual to evaluate both their conscious and unconscious insights to reach the best decision.

Excessive energy in this chakra can cause difficulties with concentration, headaches, nightmares and even hallucinations. An overactive third eye chakra can also, in some cases, lead to severe emotional disturbances, such as schizophrenia. Deficiencies show themselves as poor memory, eye problems, difficulty recognizing problems, and not being able to visualize well. In the modern world we often suffer from these problems due to the busy lives we lead. Too much time looking at computer screens, social media and rushing from here to there can affect our ability to focus or switch off. Having time away from these all-encompassing technologies and just sitting with yourself can recharge your third eye chakra and, in turn, help you when you need to concentrate, relax or sleep.

# The yantra and associated deities

The lotus flower of the Ajna yantra has only two white petals, which sit on each side of a white circle. These are variously represented as wings, our physical eyes and the topmost point where the Ida and Pingala *nadis* (channels) that carry our *prana* (life force) meet. This reminds us of the duality in all things – the highest point at which our rising vitality and our descending energy meet. The white circle represents the void, which exists beyond the five senses. Inside the circle, a crescent moon represents the Ajna vortex and a red dot shows how the body is able to rise above the sexual energy of the body symbolized by the upside down triangle below. The triangle also symbolizes wisdom, the yoni (female sexual organ) and the trinity of the godhead. Inside it is the symbol of the mantra, om, and a lingam (male sexual organ). Deities associated with this yantra are Shiva and Hakini Shakti, the aspect of the feminine divine linked to this chakra.

## The bija (seed) mantra

Om (pronounced 'aum') is the most renowned and expansive of the bija mantras. It is the mantra of assent and the form of creation, causing energy to surge upward and outward. It is used with the sixth chakra because chanting it is said to be able to open the third eye by physically merging the left and right hemispheres of the brain. According to Paramahansa Yogananda (author of *Autobiography of a Yogi*). 'Om or Aum of the *Vedas* became the sacred word *Hum* of the Tibetans, *Amin* of the Muslims and *Amen* of the Egyptians, Greeks, Romans, Jews and Christians.' The word has been translated into many different languages, cultures and religious traditions, but the creative and transformative power of the sound remains the same.

# Meditations

Meditation is the most effective way of opening the third eye chakra. But people have different reactions to the process. Some experience flashing images of things they are familiar with: nature, waterfalls, people and trains, for example. Others describe it as being able to see your thoughts, almost as if they are scrolling by on a blackboard.

It is common to have a headache during your first attempts to activate the third eye. Don't worry – as you continue to practice the headaches will go away. To train yourself to more fully appreciate the third eye, try focusing on one particular image. It could be a number, it could be an object – just try to keep your mind centered on whatever image you have chosen.

If you aren't able to get in touch with the third eye immediately, don't worry. Meditation can take a while to get used to, and activating the third eye even longer.

1  Sit down in comfortable manner for meditation. Slowly blink your eyes closed. Take a few long and deep breaths. As you exhale, bring your attention to the centre of your forehead, in between the brows and just above the brow line, and imagine an indigo-blue chakra. Watch as the dark indigo glow of the chakra illuminates your mind and then spreads to the rest of your body.

2  Imagine an entrance to your mind through the third eye. Open the door and walk into an empty room. Imagine the room any way you like – choose the color, decor, look and feel. Make it suit your tastes perfectly, so that it becomes your personal sanctuary.

3  Find the most comfortable spot in the room and sit down. Look out onto the world from there. Bring into focus the same thoughts, issues, situations and ideas that occupy your day-to-day life. Silently contemplate them.

4  Now imagine your sixth chakra spinning and gaining strength. As it spins faster, its indigo light washes over you and pervades every cell, every pore in your body.

5 Breathe deeply and feel the energy bursting from your third eye as rays of dazzling deep blue light.

6 Rest in this awareness for a few moments, gazing at the world in this new, clean light.

7 When you are finished, gently stand up and walk to the door through which you entered the room. Walk out and look back at your inner sanctuary and feel one with it before closing the door. Then imagine returning to your body. Breathe.

8 When you are ready, blink your eyes open, stand up and get on with your day.

1   Sit down in a comfortable position for meditation. Slowly blink your eyes closed. Keep your head up, your chest open and your back straight. Place your hands in your lap or your knees.

2   Breathe in and out. Be mindful of your body and how it feels in the moment. If there are aches in your body, work on relaxing those before you begin. Focus on each part of your body in turn as you sit and relax.

3   When you are ready, focus on the present moment. Feel your body expand and contract with each breath. Be aware of how your breath goes in and out. Try to focus entirely on your breathing. Take a deep breath (inhale for a count of three, then exhale for a count of three), repeat with two more deep breaths.

4   When you are ready, start focusing on your third eye at the centre of your forehead. Under your eyelids, move your eyes up toward the third eye. Keep them focused there throughout the meditation. Begin counting backwards from one hundred.

5   By the time you have reached zero, you should be ready to access the third eye. If you are properly focused, everything will be dark except the third eye. Your brain will be relaxed but functioning at a new level. Both sides of the brain will be working together and you will be aware of the energy around you.

6   You can also tell if your third eye has been activated when you are able to focus strongly on just one object and your mind is completely consumed by holding that image. Stay in that moment for a while.

7   When you are ready, bring yourself slowly out of the meditation. Move your eyes away from the third eye. Stay relaxed, but become more aware of your breath. Be mindful of the way that your breath goes in and out. Sometimes counting helps to put more focus on your breath as you are coming out of your meditation. Blink your eyes open and return to your day.

# Seventh Chakra Sahasrara

COMMON NAME
**The crown chakra**

LOCATION
**The top of the head**

ELEMENT
**Thought**

COLOR
**Violet**

SENSE
**None**

BIJA (SEED) MANTRA
**Silence/Om**

YANTRA SYMBOL
**1,000-petaled lotus flower, the petals, of different colors, are arranged in 20 layers with 50 petals in each layer. Inside is an upward-pointing triangle**

ASSOCIATED DEITIES
**Shiva, Shakti**

GEMS AND STONES
**Sapphire, amethyst, celestite**

The seventh and last chakra, Sahasrara, is unlike the others in several ways. Most importantly, it sits outside the body and is therefore not directly associated with the physical. Some say it sits on top of the head, others that it is slightly above, both descriptions explain its common name of the crown chakra. Unlike the other chakras, Sahasrara does not affect specific aspects of our lives. If your seventh chakra is unbalanced you are unlikely to notice any physical symptoms. Unlike the others, healing this chakra does not require a difficult yoga *asana*, or the chanting of a specific mantra (although some associate om with Sahasrara). Instead it requires nothing but silence, meditation and patient waiting…

This is also the hardest chakra to introduce to the beginner. For many, in this task-focused modern digital age, talk of spiritual development, enlightenment and living in a state of pure awareness can be hard to take seriously. It can be difficult to reconcile the pursuit of awareness of a higher consciousness with the demands of our daily lives. Cynicism is the most likely response. But you can think about it in another way. In our own ways, we have all had moments of joy, of extreme happiness, of clarity, of contentment. Can these not be described as 'moments of pure awareness'? Practicing meditation, prayer if you want to do it, and daily silence are disciplines that lead to increased moments of spiritual connection and longer moments of pure awareness. The more you practice these, the better you will get.

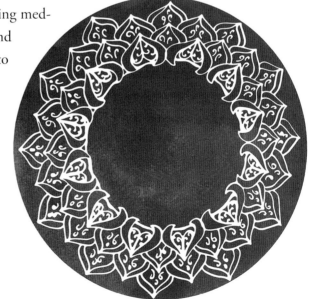

# The brain, the mind and the universe

Because of its location on top of the head, the crown chakra is closely associated with the brain and the endocrine system, notably the pineal and pituitary glands. The endocrine system is the collection of glands that produce hormones regulating growth and development, tissue function, metabolism, sexual function, reproduction, sleep and mood among other things. The brain is the centre of the nervous system. Physiologically, it works like a big computer, processing information that it receives from the senses and the body, and sending messages back to the body. It is the most complex organ in the human body and exerts centralized control over all the other organs.

The brain's statistics are astonishing: it contains approximately 86 billion nerve cells (neurons), each one capable of transmitting 1,000 impulses per second, which travel at the same speed as Formula One cars. A piece of brain tissue the size of a grain of sand contains 100,000 neurons and a billion synapses, all communicating with each other. There are 100,000 miles of blood vessels in the brain – the distance around the world at the equator is 24,900 miles! The brain plays a key role in how we are able to pay attention, our perception, awareness, thought, memory and language. But even these facts pale into insignificance when you think that the brain contains your consciousness. Your consciousness is made up of everything you have experienced in your life: your memories, your loves, your likes and dislikes, and the knowledge that one day it will end. It is astonishing to think that, at every moment, you carry everything with you inside your head. Your mind has no limits, no time constraints, no connection to the material world and no locality. Sahasrara represents that freedom – no wonder we should look after it.

# Internal quiet

Experiencing Sahasrara is a rare thing. But looking for, and finding, quiet moments of liberation, love, contentment and even bliss less so, and that too is Sahasrara. In today's fractured world, finding moments like these has become more and more important. To find this 'bliss', we need to silence the chatter (*vrittis*) in our minds; we need to cultivate an internal quiet. This does not come easily.

The crown chakra is associated with the following psychological and behavioral characteristics:

⋄ Consciousness
⋄ Awareness of higher consciousness, knowledge of what is sacred
⋄ Connection with the formless, the limitless
⋄ Realization
⋄ Liberation from limiting patterns
⋄ Communion with higher states of consciousness: ecstasy and bliss
⋄ Presence

Keeping it in balance is therefore essential for our well-being, spiritual and otherwise. For some, this chakra is the gateway to the cosmic self or the divine self, to universal consciousness. It's linked to the infinite, the universal. For others, it is a state of pure happiness and contentment. For some, Sahasrara has been lost; for others it has always been here, all we need to do is search for it.

A balanced seventh chakra allows us access to the utmost clarity and enlightened wisdom. Its energy is able to generate a blissful union with all that exists. This is regarded as spiritual ecstasy. However, an imbalance in this chakra can manifest itself as a feeling of disconnection to the spirit, a cynical attitude to what is sacred, a disconnection from the body, from earthly matters and an attitude of closed-mindedness.

Help is at hand to restore this chakra to balance through meditation and yoga. But a very effective alternative exists in the form of *pranayama* (alternate nostril breathing).

1   Sit in a comfortable position, either on a chair or on the floor, perhaps in your favored position for meditation.

2   Place your left hand on your left thigh or knee and move your right hand up towards your face. Rest your index and middle fingers at the third eye.

3   Place your thumb on your right nostril and inhale through the left nostril. Hold your breath for 2–3 seconds. Now close the left nostril with your last two fingers and release and exhale from the right nostril. Again, inhale from the right, close the right nostril with the thumb and then exhale from the left. Repeat the procedure 5–7 times on each side.

# The yantra and associated deities

The yantra for the seventh chakra is unlike any of the others. In Sanskrit, the name *sahasrara*, means 'thousandfold', and the lotus used here is said to have a thousand petals. The petals, arranged in 20 layers with 50 petals in each, come in all the colors of the rainbow. In some versions, the lotus appears to be bell-shaped, almost hat-like; in others, it is depicted simply as a circle. The lotus has been a potent emblem in India for more than two thousand years. The plant grows in muddy water and bursts into bloom when it rises to the surface, symbolizing human growth and the nurturing of our spiritual selves as we rise towards the sun.

## The bija (seed) mantra

For some, the seventh chakra has no mantra, and is best opened through silent meditation. For others, like the sixth chakra, Ajna, the seventh is associated with the mantra om. This is said to help cultivate a connection with the spirit and the whole universe or higher power. It can also help to reduce over-attachment to material things and the physical world. Some believe it stimulates the pituitary gland in the brain.

There are four parts to the seed mantra om. They are: 'ahh', 'ooo' and 'mmm' and the silence that follows. 'Ahh' represents the start of the universe. As you vibrate with it, you could feel it above your stomach. 'Ooo' represents the energy of the universe and you will feel its vibrations in your chest. 'Mmm' represents transformation. As you vibrate the sound, you should feel it in your brain. The last sound, when the long 'mmm' has ceased, takes us into the deep silence of the Infinite, the Void itself, that of Infinite Consciousness.

# Meditations

1 Sit in a comfortable place for meditation. Take a long and deep breath. As you exhale, move your attention to the top of your head and imagine a violet chakra. The dark violet glow of the chakra illuminates your mind and your body.

2 Imagine a big, white lotus with its petals closed in the same place as your crown chakra. Look at the lotus and contemplate its shape, color and texture.

3 As you pay attention, the lotus slowly starts to swirl along with the chakra.

4 One by one the petals of the lotus start to open. As the first layer flowers, you see un-countable rows of more petals still to open.

5 With every new petal opening the lotus starts spinning faster. You realize that every such opening leads to yet another layer of closed petals. The blooming of the lotus is a process of infinite stages.

6 Now see your seventh chakra spinning with equal strength. The chakra's violet light washes over you and fills every cell, every pore of your body.

7 Breathe deeply and feel the energy from your crown chakra connecting you to the sky above and to the earth below, and to everything in between, so you become one with existence.

8 Rest in this awareness.

9 When you are ready, blink your eyes open and stand up ready for the rest of your day.

* * *

1   If you can, find a quiet place outside, in the garden, on the roof, somewhere private. In the evening or the night would be preferable. Take a candle or a torch of some kind to help you find your way. If you cannot, then indoors will be fine too.

2   Sit down in a comfortable position for meditation. Place your right hand over your heart, and let fingertips of your left hand graze the ground beside you. Close your eyes. Settle into your seat, feeling the solidity of the ground beneath you, the support of your connection to the earth. Out of that support, allow your spine to rise, the crown of your head to soar into the heavens.

3   Connect to the flow of your breath. Feel the sacred quality of that connection – this process of inhale and exhale that is with you for the duration of this body's time here.

4   Sensing each rise and fall – each coming and going – in its fullness, ask yourself, 'Where does this breath come from?'

5   Is it possible for you to consider that, as you breathe in and out, a force beyond you is providing the very breath to you which sustains your life? It is within you and all around you. It is the stuff of everything, and beyond this body and this life. Can you be open to such a possibility?

6   If you can, allow yourself to name this force in your life: Spirit, Mother, God, Love... Contemplate this presence... What might it look like to you, feel like to you? When do you feel most connected to the sacred?

7   When you are ready, bring your attention back to your breath. Exist in your breathing. Then, gently blink your eyes open, move your fingers, arms and legs, and stand up. After a moment or two, you can get up and carry on with your evening.

# Moving into balance

Caring for yourself, for your body, for your spirit, for your mental and physical health, starts with awareness. Awareness of your lifestyle, the things you eat and drink, how much you exercise, your ethics and morals, and so on. It is important that we choose how we want to live our lives. Of course, no one chooses to suffer ill health, but life does inflict wear-and-tear on both body and mind, whatever lifestyle we choose.

As we have seen, chakras have been a part of people's lives for over 2,000 years and, if you have read this far, you have now joined that group. By now you will have developed an awareness of the seven major chakras, and by meditating on them, as described in the chapters on the individual chakras, you will have been able to open them up and begin to develop an awareness of how they feel, how they might affect you, and whether they are balanced or not. In this section, we are going to look more closely on how to develop a regular care regime for them and how to heal or realign them if they become unbalanced or blocked.

We have already examined the benefits of meditation in your regular chakra care, and it is a good idea to start any session on chakras with a few moments of meditation, perhaps combined with some appropriate mantra chants. In terms of healing, yoga poses, which are often known by the Sanskrit word *asanas*, are by far the most effective method. The chakras have been linked with the practice of yoga since the 10th century bce, a connection that is still holding strong. This is thought to be because the practice of bending, stretching and twisting *asanas* helps our energy and life-force (*prana*) flow through our bodies.

Undertaken regularly, yoga is likely to keep your chakras well balanced. For this purpose, they are best done in order (starting at the bottom and moving up the spine) one after the other. However, if you should develop a blockage, the healing *asanas* that follow have been chosen with each specific chakra in mind to help you target any one for particular attention.

***Note:*** Yoga should be taken seriously. Done incorrectly or inappropriately, it can result in injury. The best way to practice it is to join a reputable school or join a class run by an accredited yoga teacher. If you are pregnant, recovering from an operation, suffer from back pain, high blood pressure, heart problems, unsteady blood pressure or sugar levels, or are recovering from a hip, knee or back fracture, you should not be attempting to practice these poses.

If you feel any pain when practicing any of them, please stop immediately. Never push your body beyond its natural limits in any pose. If in doubt, please go to your doctor for advice.

# Balance the chakras with yoga

You need to do a little preparation for a yoga session. Much of this will be the same as for a meditation session, but it is helpful to remind yourself of these things before you start so that you are not interrupted or disturbed. Find a quiet and preferably uncluttered room in your home for yoga practice. Dress in comfortable clothes, in which you can move easily. Tracksuit bottoms, leggings and a T-shirt are ideal. Yoga is always practiced in bare feet. It is essential that you have a yoga mat.

You may have demands on your time that dictate when you can do yoga, but with the rays of the early morning sun coming through the window would be ideal. Open the window to let in some fresh air if appropriate. Plan to do your session before a meal rather than afterwards, make sure you listen to the call of nature before you start. Drink a little water, if you are thirsty. You are now ready to warm-up.

Start with a simple breathing practice. The exercise below is designed to encourage even, steady breaths.

# Breath awareness

1 Sit on a chair, placing your feet on the ground, hip-width apart, with your knees directly above. If your feet don't reach the floor, use books or blocks to support them. Alternatively, sit on the floor cross-legged if you are comfortable doing so, using a firm cushion to sit on so that your back does not collapse. You can also place supports under your knees if they are uncomfortable.

2 For either seated position, gently press the sitting bones down and lengthen the spine so it is upright but not rigid. Relax the shoulders down away from the ears. Rest your hands on your lap. Gently close your eyes if you are comfortable doing so; otherwise half-close them and cast your gaze softly downwards.

3 Mentally scan your body from the head downwards, noticing any areas where you are holding tension – the facial muscles, the shoulders, the abdominal area. Equally notice areas that feel open and relaxed, not tense. Notice all the different sensations of the body.

4 Now bring your awareness to your breath. Without trying to change it, start to observe the quality of the breath – the texture, the rhythm, the speed. Is the inbreath shorter or longer than the outbreath? Notice all the varying sensations of the breath as it flows in and out of your body.

5 Watch each breath for its duration, observing with acceptance (rather than frustration if it doesn't meet your expectations).

**6** After a few minutes, start to follow your outbreath from its start to its end. Notice whether you allow it to run all the way to the end, or whether you curtail it and start breathing in before you have fully breathed out. If this is the case, see if you can allow the outbreath to reach its natural conclusion.

**7** Be patient and don't worry if it's not possible. It is a process. The most important thing is for the breath to be natural and not forced.

**8** Notice how the navel moves towards the spine towards the end of the outbreath, and how there is a natural pause at the end of the outbreath if you allow it to take place.

**9** Notice how the next inbreath arises out of this pause and how the inhalation will deepen naturally as a result of the fuller outbreath.

**10** Follow the breath for a few minutes and when you are ready to end the practice, slowly bring your awareness back and start to gently move the arms, legs, fingers and toes before standing up.

After the breathing exercise, give yourself a few moments to gather your thoughts. When you are ready, the following *asana* will help you engage the chakras in preparation for the particular healing pose or poses you wish to practice. If you are a complete beginner or unsteady on your feet, then you can try it sitting in a chair. Use a chair that offers firm support. If you are going to use a chair, you must ensure that your feet are firmly on the ground, hip-width apart, and your knees are in line with your ankles.

# Tadasana
# (Mountain pose)

1 Stand with your feet hip-width apart. Ensure your feet are in line with each other.

2 Root down with the heels and the balls of your feet, spread and extend your toes, draw up the foot arches.

3 Draw your knees and thigh muscles upwards.

4 Press the top of the inner thighs back and the tailbone forward. Draw the lower abdomen and navel in and up.

5 Lengthen the spine upwards, lift the breastbone, allowing the shoulders to relax back and down; broaden the chest.

6 Lift the crown of the head up while pressing the soles of the feet down, particularly the heels and the mounds of the toes, into the ground.

7 Extend your arms down the sides of the body, palms facing your thighs. Gaze straight ahead and breathe steadily. Remain in the pose for 20 seconds.

# Root chakra healing pose
# Vrksasana (Tree pose)

1 Stand in Tadasana (see page 77).

2 Put your weight on your left foot; raise your right leg and bend it at the knee. Place your raised foot on the inner thigh or the inner shin of your left leg. (Avoid placing the foot on the inner knee.) Your toes should be pointing downwards.

3 Join your palms together at the heart (as in prayer position).

4 If you feel unstable, place a hand on the wall for support.

5 Let your spine lengthen upwards as you press the foot of your standing leg firmly down.

6 Feel the sense of being grounded as you root down.

7 Gaze straight ahead at eye level. This will help you to balance.

8 Stay as long as feels comfortable and then return to Tadasana.

9 Repeat on the other side.

*'Like a tree you have to find your roots,*
*and then you can bend in the wind'*
Angela Farmer

# Sacral chakra healing pose
# Utkata Konasana (Goddess pose)

1  Stand in Tadasana (see page 77).

2  Step your feet wide apart (about 3–4 feet, depending on your height). Turn your toes slightly out.

3  Start to bend your knees, extending them in the same direction as your toes. Make sure your knees are correctly aligned and not collapsing inwards.

4  Lower your hips down to the height of your knees, if possible, but only go as far as feels comfortable. Take the tailbone slightly forwards and lengthen the spine upwards, keeping the torso as upright as possible.

5  Press down evenly on the soles of the feet.

6  Extend your arms out to the sides at shoulder height. Bend your arms at the elbows so that your palms face forwards, the fingers upwards, to form a right angle.

7  If you have a shoulder injury, rest your hands on your thighs.

8  Stay in the pose for 20–30 seconds, or as long as feels comfortable, then press through the feet in order to come up. Then bring the feet back together.

# Navel chakra healing pose
# Virabhadrasana (Warrior I pose)

**1** Stand in Tadasana (see page 77).

**2** Turn to the side of mat, extend your feet approximately 3–4 feet apart.

**3** Raise your arms above your head, palms facing each other. Yours arms should be straight and shoulder-width apart. (If your shoulders are tight or uncomfortable, take your arms wider apart.)

**4** Turn your right foot 90 degrees to the right, turn your back foot in to the right.

**5** Bend your right knee. Your right knee should be positioned over your right heel, not collapsing inwards and not going beyond the heel.

**6** Press down on your left outer heel; press your inner left thigh back; take your tailbone forwards. Stretch your body upwards. Gaze straight ahead.

**7** Hold for 15–20 seconds, then come up out of the pose. Repeat on other side.

# Heart chakra healing pose Bhujangasana (Cobra pose)

1   Lie prone (front-side down) on the floor.

2   Stretch your legs back and press the front of your thighs and feet into the ground. Draw your tailbone to the ground.

3   Place your hands flat on the floor by the sides of your chest with your elbows hugging the sides of your body.

4   On an inhalation, start to lift your chest off the ground by pressing your hands firmly down and starting to straighten the arms.

5   Draw the navel up towards the chest, drop the shoulders down away from the ears, lift the sternum without the front ribs flaring.

6   Ensure the backbend is evenly distributed throughout the spine to avoid putting pressure on the lower back.

7   Do not strain the back by trying to come up too high. Keeping the elbows bent rather than straightening the arms completely will help avoid any potential strain.

8   Stay in the pose for up to 30 seconds, then, on an exhalation, lower your body down and rest.

# Throat chakra healing pose
# Setu Bandha Sarvangasana
# (Bridge pose)

1  Lie supine (on your back) on the ground, and bend your knees and place your feet firmly on the ground with your heels directly under your knees; your feet should be parallel and hip-width apart.

2  Extend your arms by the side of your body, palms face-down. Press the arms into the ground.

3  Press down with your feet to lift your hips slowly off the ground using your arms for support. Extend your tailbone towards the knees to lengthen your lower back; then lift a little more (never forcing) and move your chest in the direction of your chin.

4  Check that your thighs remain parallel, lifting your outer hips up and releasing your inner thighs down towards the floor.

5  Remain in this position for approximately 30 seconds, or as long as feels comfortable, and then slowly come down.

# Third eye chakra healing pose
# Balasana (Child's pose)

1  Kneel down on all fours.

2  Your knees should be slightly more than hip-width apart. Bring your big toes together. Move your sitting bones back to rest on your heels. You can place a rolled-up blanket or towel under your feet if there is discomfort in the front of the feet, and/or, similarly, between the backs of your thighs and your calves if your sitting bones don't reach your heels.

3  On an exhalation, bend forward from the hips, keeping the front of your body long, and rest your torso between your thighs.

4  Place your forehead on the ground, or, if it does not reach the ground, rest your forehead on a block (or book). Your head should not hang without support. Observe the place where your forehead meets the ground or support.

5  Extend your arms out in front of you, palms face-down.

6  This is a resting pose – there should be no discomfort in your knees, legs, shoulders or back. Let your breath be easy and fluid.

7  Rest in this position for up to 2 minutes.

8  Exit the pose on an inhalation, pressing your hands into the floor to lift up your body.

# Crown chakra healing pose
# Savasana (Corpse pose)

This is an excellent exercise to rebalance the crown chakra, but it can also be used to finish any chakra healing session.

1   Sit on the floor, extend your legs out in front of you and slowly lower yourself to the ground until you are lying supine.

2   Let your arms and legs fall away from the sides of your body. Turn your palms to face the ceiling, let your legs and feet relax out to the sides. Ensure your limbs are as symmetrical as possible to enable optimal relaxation.

3   Place a pillow under your knees if there is any tension in your back or, alternatively, you can support the lower legs on the seat of a chair.

4   Place a folded blanket under your head and neck if your head is tilted backwards.

5   Close your eyes and allow your body to relax; surrender the weight of the body to the ground beneath you.

6   Keep your attention on your breathing, and try to remain completely still.

7   Stay in the pose for up to 5 minutes, then slowly bring your awareness back, open your eyes, draw your knees up and over to the right and then push yourself up to a seated position.

# Feeding the Chakras

Keeping your energy points in balance is helped by a healthy diet. The best diets are based around a little meat – if you are a carnivore – plus vegetables, grains and fruits. We are all encouraged to 'eat the rainbow' and this is a philosophy based on Ayurveda, the 'science of life', a system used in India for thousands of years to bring the body into a healthy and vitalized state of balance. Food of certain colors encourages healing within your body. Choosing foods of those colors that are in tune with the colors of the chakras, the cycles of the seasons, and the time of the day will help develop a calm and nourished body. Spend a bit of time choosing the freshest meat, vegetables and fruit you can.

## MULADHARA

The root chakra is represented by the color red, for energy. If you are feeling run-down, fatigued, burnt-out, lazy or lethargic, red foods such as tomatoes, strawberries, raspberries, radishes, pumpkin and beetroot will help to boost your energy levels and your body temperature. Also choose root vegetables, such as carrots, potatoes and parsnips, as well as onions and garlic. Protein-rich foods, like eggs, meat, beans, tofu, soy products and peanut butter will also bring benefits. Cook with spices like paprika and pepper.

## SVADHISTHANA

The sacral chakra, also known as the creativity chakra, is located at the navel and associated with the color orange. It governs your confidence and self-worth, so if you are low on these and feel unworthy of love then eat sweet fruits like mangoes, melons and oranges. Vegetables such as carrots, sweet potatoes and butternut squash will also help you regain control and balance in your life. Honey and nuts are also recommended. For cooking, use spices like cinnamon and vanilla to add flavor.

## MANIPURA

This is called the solar plexus chakra, affects your ego and self-esteem, and is represented by the color yellow. Yellow food is a natural mood enhancer, so if you are sad or depressed, eat fruit like pineapple or bananas, or vegetables such as corn on the cob or yellow peppers. Dairy products, like milk, cheese and yogurt are also helpful, as are grains such as rice, cereals, flax and sunflower seeds. Robust spices, such as ginger, mint, turmeric and cumin will flavor your cooking, along with more subtle flavors from chamomile and fennel.

## ANAHATA

The heart chakra, associated with matters of love, of course, is also affected by stress, fatigue and acidity. Its color is green and the healing process can be helped by eating leafy vegetables, such as spinach, broccoli, cauliflower, cabbage and kale. You could even put them in the juicer for a healthy breakfast drink. Either that or serve up a big salad with the tastiest leaves you can find, adding some avocado and grapes along with basil, thyme and coriander. Green tea during the day can also help in rejuvenating a steady emotional frame of mind.

## VISHUDDHA

This chakra is associated with the throat, and represents our power and responsibility through the way we communicate. If this chakra is blocked we might have difficulty in expressing ourselves, perhaps because of a cold, a sore throat or an ear infection. It is associated with the colors blue and black, and a healthy bowl of blueberries or blackberries is sure to hit the spot. Tree fruits, such as apples, pears, peaches and plums, are also helpful. To soothe a sore throat, drink water, fruit juice and herbal tea.

## AJNA

The third eye, as it is popularly known, is located in the centre of the brow of your head, just above the eyebrows. It is the seat of wisdom, intuition and perspective and can therefore be vulnerable to frustration and anger when out of balance. Feed it with foods that are calming such as chocolate, maybe washed down with a little red wine. This chakra's color is indigo so try cooking some purple foods, such as aubergines, make a salad with radicchio, or go for a simple plate of fresh grapes, plums and figs. You can also boost the flavors of your cooking with allspice, cardamom or sage.

## SAHASRARA

The highest form of chakra, called the crown chakra, represents your higher self and opens up your communication with the universe. In general, this chakra does not need feeding, instead benefitting from fasting or detoxifying, which can help in awakening spiritual communication. In addition, burning incense such as copal, frankincense and juniper can help cleanse the air around you and nourish the chakra as you meditate.

# Healing the Chakras

Yoga, meditation and a selective diet are not the only options open to those wanting to maintain the health and balance of their energy centers. The use of essential oils, energy healing techniques, gems and crystals are also widespread, particularly when it comes to healing. This might be by: clearing unwanted energy, like stress, from the system; dissolving blockages, such as pain or tension; increasing the flow of vitality through the body; or even increasing one particular type of positive energy when you need it, like calm or optimism. But do they really work?

## Essential oils

Essential oils are aromatic compounds found in the leaves, flowers, roots, stems, bark and seeds of plants. They have been in use since the age of Ancient Egypt, for therapeutic, cosmetic and ceremonial purposes, offering the promise of improvement of both mood and health. In plants, the oils serve various functions: assisting pollination, repelling pests and predators, fighting disease and encouraging cell regeneration. For humans, their use is effective in the short and long term, as an aid to physical wellness, supporting massage, yoga and meditation, clearing chakras of unwanted energy, and maintaining emotional balance among other things.

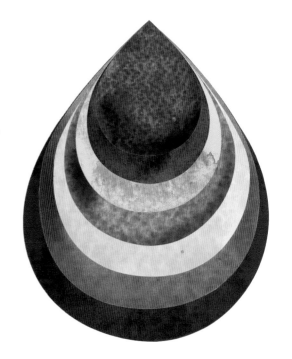

There is scientific proof of this. Essential oils are antibacterial, antiviral, antifungal, antioxidant, sedative, analgesic, antispasmodic, cleansing and antimicrobial. Because of their tiny molecular size, and because they are fat-soluble, essential oils can penetrate cell membranes and can therefore pass from the blood into the brain fluid in the central nervous system. Oils can disrupt viruses and repair damaged cell replication. They can clean receptor sites leading to improved cell communication, re-program DNA, and deliver oxygen to tissues. They are also used to treat bacteria, such as MRSA, blood clots, stress and disease-causing free radicals. They are known to calm moods, help with relaxation, and improve sleep. It is estimated that 25 per cent of commercially available medicines contain plant derivatives. They are used in a number of commercially available products, such as personal-care items, household cleaners, aromatherapy candles and mosquito repellents.

Essential oils enter the body through the nose, skin and mouth, from where they will reach the bloodstream. These multiple methods make oils easy to use for adults and children. Perhaps the most common use is through the nose. Many people use a diffuser to scent a room creating a range of atmospheres, though they are also useful to inhibit airborne bacteria and help those with breathing difficulties. For an instant hit, you can simply put a drop of oil in the palm of your hand, rub both hands together, and breathe it in deeply. Because oils can be calming, soothing and energizing, and because they have easy access to the brain, this is a fast and easy way to affect mood. Essential oils are often diffused in clinics and hospitals because of their calming properties.

Because of their molecular make-up, these oils penetrate the skin quickly, having an instant, localized effect. This kind of application is good for occasional pain, muscle aches, headaches, acne, bruising, burns, rashes and as insect repellent.

These oils can be very strong and are often diluted with a 'carrier' or 'base' oil, such as coconut or almond oil. It is important that you read the labels on any essential oil products to understand the recommended dilution for your purpose. It is particularly important that you do this if you have sensitive skin or are using the oils with children or infants (see note below). They are also a wonderful aid for massage, particularly chakra massage. It is believed that our thoughts and actions are absorbed through each chakra. When negative energy flows through a chakra it begins to spin too fast or too slow, making it unbalanced. This can affect us physically, emotionally and spiritually. Massage, reflection, meditation and energy work using essential oils can help restore balance to each of the chakras. There are a number of essential oils that resonate with each chakra. Here is a recommended starter list:

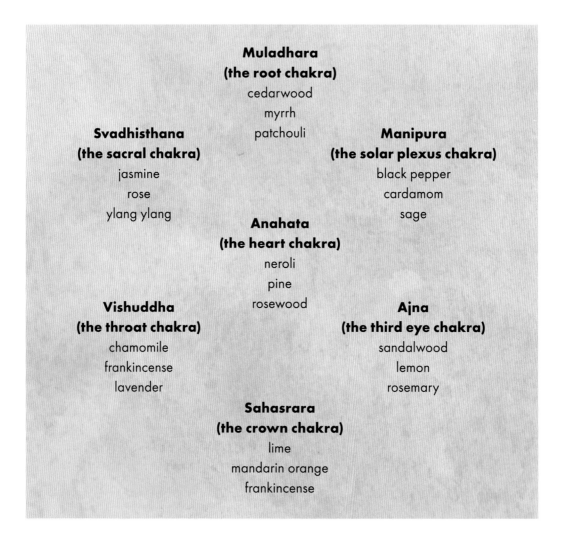

**Muladhara**
**(the root chakra)**
cedarwood
myrrh
patchouli

**Svadhisthana**
**(the sacral chakra)**
jasmine
rose
ylang ylang

**Manipura**
**(the solar plexus chakra)**
black pepper
cardamom
sage

**Anahata**
**(the heart chakra)**
neroli
pine
rosewood

**Vishuddha**
**(the throat chakra)**
chamomile
frankincense
lavender

**Ajna**
**(the third eye chakra)**
sandalwood
lemon
rosemary

**Sahasrara**
**(the crown chakra)**
lime
mandarin orange
frankincense

Though it is much rarer, some oils can be ingested. For example, peppermint oil has been found to be effective in combatting the effects of Irritable Bowel Syndrome (IBS). However, a number of essential oils are not only extremely strong, they are also toxic. It is also true to say that, like medicines, they can affect people in different ways. So, the advice is **do not ingest essential oils** unless you do so under the advice and guidance of a trained herbalist.

Essential oils have their critics, of course. They can be expensive because of the labour-intensive work involved in producing them. They are wasteful, for example, it takes 13.5 kilos of lavender flowers to make a 15ml bottle of essential oil. They have potential side effects, which could be serious for babies and pets, and they are unregulated. Please consider the following warning before you consider using them:

*Important to note:* Essential oils are very strong. If you are pregnant or are intending to use them on children under 12, it is recommended that you visit your doctor to ask for advice.

If you have sensitive skin and are using an oil for the first time, you should do a skin sensitivity test first. Put a few drops of diluted oil on your inner thigh and wait 24 hours to see if any irritation or redness occurs.

Avoid application on sensitive areas, like the eyes, genitals, inner ears and anywhere you have broken skin. The best places for application are the bottom of the feet, the wrists and the back of the neck. Massage after application increases the blood flow and maximises oil absorption.

# Energy healing

Energy healing is any therapy that uses the energy of the human body to bring the body back into balance so that it can begin to heal itself. Given that these techniques use the body's life-force (*prana* in Hindu practices, *qi* in Chinese medicine), they are closely associated with the chakra energy centers. There are a number of different schools of thought in this area, but those most relevant to the study of the chakras are reiki, reflexology, acupuncture, color and sound therapy.

Reiki is a Japanese practice that was developed by Dr Mikao Usui in the early years of the 20th century. A Reiki healer uses the palm of their hands, without touching the patient, and uses their own body as a channel to direct universal energy into the patient. During a session, the healer's hands are placed in the energetic, sometimes called auric, field over the location of all seven major chakras, usually starting with the crown chakra. Healers are taught not to direct the energy, just to let it flow where it is needed. Reflexology works on the basis that there are pressure points in the feet and the palms of the hands that relate to different parts of the body, and that working with these pressure points can help to ease problems in the associated bodily areas. For maintaining chakra balance, the most important of these is an area right the way along the arch of the foot, which controls our spinal reflexes. Thirty seconds of massage on each foot should restore the balance.

Acupuncture originated in China and has become a popular form of alternative healing around the world. The practice involves fine needles being inserted into the skin at various defined points around the body in order to balance the flow of *qi*. Western doctors tend to view the practice as a way to increase blood flow by stimulating the nerves, muscles and connective tissue in various parts of the body rather than proper medicine. But research has shown that acupuncture is helpful in the treatment of headaches, hypertension, depression, back pain, nausea, rheumatoid arthritis and other conditions.

Color is simply light of varying wavelengths and frequencies. Electromagnetic waves constantly surround us, and color is part of those waves. Every single cell in the body needs light energy. Our cells absorb color, and this affects us on every level: physically, emotionally and spiritually. It is thought that the colors of the rainbow: red, yellow, green, blue, orange, violet and indigo resonate with the chakras, the body's main energy centers. Color therapy is the practice of visualising the relevant color, along with repeated exposure to that color, wearing clothes of that color and eating foods of that color in order to speed up healing processes.

Sound healing, also known as vibrational healing, is believed to date back to Ancient Greece. The basic principle behind it is that the entire universe is in a state of vibration. This includes every organ, cell, bone, tissue and liquid of the human body, and the electromagnetic fields that surround it. If we are not resonating with some part of ourselves or our surroundings, we become dissonant and therefore unhealthy, our naturally healthy frequency becomes a frequency that vibrates without harmony, creating illness. Sound healing might involve listening to music or other sounds, singing, dancing, meditation or playing an instrument in order to restore the harmonic vibrations we need to restore our physical and emotional well-being.

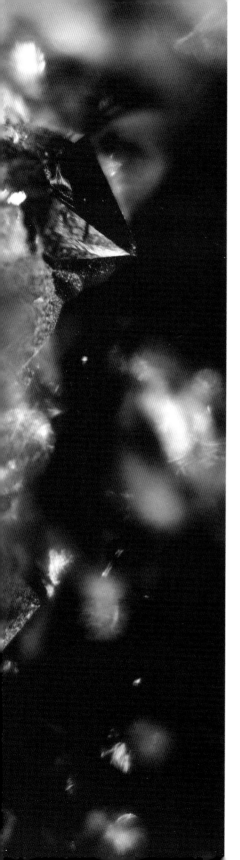

# Good vibrations

The ancient Egyptians believed that gemstones had the power to restore health and often buried deceased family members with them tucked into the layers of linen cloth in which their bodies were wrapped. Since then they have gone in and out of fashion, not as a healing aid for your ailments, but rather as a method of soothing the soul. Today, they are undergoing something of a resurgence in popularity. Some claim this is because in today's fast-paced world more people are turning to old traditions to relieve the stresses of everyday life. Others see gemstones and crystals as a natural antidote to the energy-suck of technology that we deal with at work and at home. However, there are also those who claim we have a sympathetic resonance with crystals, and researchers are said to have been able to detect electrical energy emanating from quartz crystals when they are placed close to a chakra. The stones must be cleansed in water and then put outside in the sunlight or moonlight which will energize them.

The basic idea is that crystals carry certain energies that can have a positive effect on our own. In a similar way to magnets, crystals and gemstones use energy to attract or repel. When you place certain stones over certain parts of your body, they interact with your individual chakras. Your energy transforms, vibrates, pulses, moves and shifts in accordance with the properties and energetic signature of the particular crystal.

As you will have read in the chapters on the individual chakras, each is associated with a number of gems and stones. These are listed as follows:

**Muladhara
(the root chakra)**
ruby
bloodstone
garnet

**Svadhisthana
(the sacral chakra)**
carnelian
fire opal
topaz

**Manipura
(the solar plexus chakra)**
topaz
yellow tourmaline
emerald

**Anahata
(the heart chakra)**
jade
peridot
rose quartz

**Vishuddha
(the throat chakra)**
blue topaz
aquamarine
lapis lazuli

**Ajna
(the third eye chakra)**
diamond
emerald
sapphire

**Sahasrara
(the crown chakra)**
sapphire
amethyst
celestite

If you were to visit a 'healing crystal' practitioner, they would most likely get you to lie down and relax before placing appropriate stones near the chakra points. This is said to realign, rebalance and reenergise the chakras back into their appropriate functions. Some suggest that you place crystals in your home or hold them in your hands while meditating or, indeed, carry them with you throughout the day.

For some, crystals have been successful in preventing headaches, relieving stress, improving mood, even bringing peace and happiness. But scientists have been unable to prove claims that they work as medicine. If you believe in them, they might make you feel better through the perception of 'good vibrations' and that perception may help alleviate some emotional or spiritual stress.

part **2**

AURAS

# The history of auras

Aura means "breeze" or "breath" in the ancient Greek language, and was also the name of a lesser-known Greek Titan goddess. The word's use as a name for the part of the energy sheath (visible to some adepts) outside the physical body came into being around the end of the 19th century. This latter meaning, of a sort of halo surrounding the body, was made particularly popular in the West by the theosophists. Theosophy is a school of philosophical thought founded in the late 19th century that focuses on examining the truth of the nature of the world and spirituality. It draws on aspects of wisdom found in Hinduism, Buddhism and Western esoteric thought.

*This mosaic of Christ in the arms of the Virgin Mary shows both with halos around their heads. There are those who believe that this is to show the purity of their auras.*

The movement has so many aspects to its practice that it would take another book to fully explore it all. However, for our purposes, we should look at the work of the theosophist called Charles Webster Leadbeater, whose illustrations appeared in Part 1 of this book.

Leadbeater wrote extensively on the makeup of the human energy body, as well as doing some very detailed sketches of his idea of what chakras (energy points) in the body look like. He drew on some ideas from the Indian subcontinent alongside his own experiences of seeing energy after having done a number of meditation practices. This work was then used as the basis of an exploration into the subject in the late 1970s by Christopher Hills. The classic seven-chakra, rainbow-colored system that you may be familiar with is the result of the work Hills did in that decade.

Beyond the work of 19th-century theosophy luminaries, we have little historical literature on auras as we know them today. However, it has been speculated that the halos shown around the heads of religious figures in Christian iconography could be there to indicate the radiant purity of their auras. Certainly the spirit or soul has been written about extensively, and some of the ideas we have of what remains after we die can be attributed to an energy body, if not precisely to an aura.

Author W.E. Butler wrote in his work *How to Read the Aura* that: "It is said in the East that the spiritual aura of the Lord Gautama Buddha extended for two hundred miles, and they also say that the whole of this planet is held in the aura of a very great Being." Could it be that the more spiritually advanced we get, our auras become beacons of radiant joy for the world around us?

# Everything is responsive

Huna is a life philosophy from Hawaii that has many beneficial ideas about the world around us. Serge Kahili King, a Huna practitioner, has spoken about a number of principles governing the nature of reality. Among them is one that is very important and useful to anyone interested in auras: "everything is alive and responsive." Everything has an aura, irrespective of whether it is animate or inanimate. It used to be thought likely that only living beings had an energetic aura, but many esoteric practitioners have now confirmed that all matter has an aura. If you stub your toe on a cupboard, it may well be that your aura and that of the cupboard are not in harmony, and the stubbed toe is the outcome. (Although, it may just be that you need to move the cupboard to a less inconvenient spot!)

If we accept that everything has an aura, and that this aura is in constant interplay with all the other auras of things, people and places with which it interacts, then you can see how important it is to ensure that you only have around you those auras that you align well with.

## PRAISE, DON'T CRITICIZE

One of the key ways in which Huna practitioners, in the tradition followed by Serge Kahili King, acknowledge the principle that everything is alive and responsive is to praise rather than criticize. This is a good way to come into harmony with all the auras of what surrounds you. A typical day might involve frustration when something doesn't work quite right. The coffee maker might not work the first time, or

the shower might not get hot because the water heater isn't working properly. This might cause you to internally (or even externally) criticize and curse the inanimate objects involved and the overall quality of your life. This will immediately put you into disharmony in both your energy body and your physical experience. It is always far better to praise or to acknowledge things that do go right. How fortunate we are to have coffee makers, hot water and indoor plumbing that gives us an abundance of flowing water.

It is unrealistic to be positive all the time, even when things are going wrong, but maintaining an "attitude of gratitude" helps you to keep your auric energy clear and encourage the auras of the things and people around you to also vibrate at that higher level. You will find, over time, that life runs far more smoothly and happily.

Self
brahman

Bliss body
anandamaya kosha

Wisdom body
*vijnanamaya kosha*

Emotion body
manomaya kosha

Energy body
pranamaya kosha

Physical body
annamaya kosha

# Energetic sheaths

Different traditions believe energy is ordered in a variety of ways within the body. Some systems believe there are seven energy bodies radiating out from the skin, each concerned with a different aspect of your physical, emotional, intellectual and spiritual makeup. However, in Vedantic philosophy there are five koshas (sheaths) in the body that surround the eternal self, called the *brahman* or *atman* in the Advaita Vedanta. These sheaths each have an important role to play in keeping a person happy and healthy; they also interact with each other so that damage to one sheath will inevitably affect all the others.

You can find out more about how to restore each of the five koshas to optimum health on pages 104–107. Once you have cleared each of these five energy sheaths, you can maintain overall health by just working with one sheath, which represents all of them. If one visualizes a core, single sheath and concentrates one's efforts on keeping this clear and strong, the health of all the layers of the energy body is maintained. As such, we shall call this composite energy field the protective sheath.

## THE PROTECTIVE SHEATH

The protective sheath reflects the energy of our current day-to-day life. If you could view it (and developing a meditation practice will help you begin to "see" with an inner eye), you would see an ever-swirling, moving mist of color at the outer edge of the shape of things and people. Those changes in the energy body can happen because of your fluctuating emotions, hormonal changes, your interactions with others and your thoughts and beliefs about yourself and others.

When this sheath is working well, your intuition will be strong about situations and other people. You will see their motivations clearly and, for some, it is almost as if you have a psychic ability to know what's coming your way. That is because you do! This sheath, which has all the qualities of the koshas, affects your psychic abilities keenly, and working to keep it clear and healthy is a good way to stay psychically alert.

If this sheath is damaged or weak, you can be left open to psychic attack. This is when you begin to attract unwelcome experiences to you, and life begins to have an increasing level of frustration to it. By working to strengthen this sheath, you can ensure you only attract those experiences to you that work for your highest good and make you feel positive and blissful about life.

# Cleansing the annamaya kosha

The annamaya kosha is also known as the physical body, or the food sheath. This is because it is your physical self, which comprises what you eat and this corporeal body, that will become food for the Earth and its creatures, once your *atman,* or soul, has left this plane of existence.

It is therefore natural that the best way to cleanse and protect this part of your energetic makeup is good nutrition and maintaining excellent physical health. You may think that the physical is not as important as the spiritual when it comes to auras, but this is not true. You reside in your body, and any discomfort here will affect all your energy sheaths.

While it is beyond the scope of this book to advise on diet, it would be beneficial to look into booking an ayurvedic session to understand your specific body type and which foods will support your overall physical health. As a general rule of thumb for everyone, avoiding processed foods and veering toward whole, organically produced foods is best. The herbalism suggestions in Part 3 will also help.

You can also cleanse this part of your auric body through exercise. However, be aware that the third leg of the tripod of physical health is relaxation, so do not undertake overly strenuous exercise. You can find some helpful yoga *asanas* to do in Part 1.

# Cleansing the pranamaya kosh

Pranamaya is the kosha that pertains to energy, since *prana* means energy. It is the vital energy that courses through the meridians or *nadis* of your body. This energy intersects at certain points called chakras, which you learned about in Part 1.

If this energy sheath is not operating at full health, you will suffer from breathing problems and may lose your sense of smell or experience chronic fatigue. Working with the breath is the best way to cleanse this kosha. A daily breathing practice is recommended for all people as being as necessary as brushing your teeth in the morning.

You can do the alternate nostril breathing exercise on page 125 as a quick and easy way to bring this sheath into alignment. Not only does this exercise restore the workings of this kosha, it also balances the "male" and "female" energies in the body, so you physically experience equilibrium. It does not matter what sex or gender you are, or how you identify yourself at all, as this is a cosmic duality at play that resides in all matter, irrespective of how it is presented biologically—we all have masculine and feminine energy as a dual experience within us which is usually resolved into one at the point of death or enlightenment.

# Cleansing the manomaya kosha

Have you ever heard the saying "energy flows to where attention goes"? This sheath, which is often called the mental or the emotional body kosha, shows the truth of that saying. Your emotions (the "energy" part of the saying) arise from your thoughts (the "attention" part of the saying), and those emotions have a direct influence on your health. Medical researchers have found that those with a positive outlook on life and optimistic thoughts live longer, healthier lives than those who are negative and pessimistic. So one of the best ways to cleanse and protect this sheath is to think good thoughts. Think well of people, and praise rather than criticise the world around you.

Another way to heal this sheath is to do anything that stops you from overthinking, so meditation, chanting and restorative yoga poses are all good for this. Since the way we think is often formed in childhood, it is very good to do the yoga *asana* Child's Pose. This helps us stop dwelling on, and feeling emotionally hurt by, thoughts of conflict or injustice. If you can put aside ideas that are causing you pain, you will heal this body and send vibrations of joy throughout your whole energy system.

# Cleansing the vijnanamaya kosha

This is where your intuition, wisdom and inspiration reside. Damage to this kosha will cause you to doubt yourself, feel unconnected to your spiritual truth, and give rise to depression and despair.

Mindfulness can help heal this sheath, since we are going beyond the world of rationality to a place of being the timeless "witness." This is the eternal part of yourself, the Buddha mind, that observes without judgment or attachment.

If you find that meditation or mindfulness does not work for you, you could try more traditional talking therapies to resolve problems in your Manomaya kosha, which will then affect the Vijnanamaya. The important thing is to go beyond the physical and to your own sense of spiritual awareness. This is the case even on a secular level, as you do not need to follow any religious or spiritual tradition to understand that energy is more than what we see in the material world. Take a quantum physics class if you really want to get a scientific understanding of what spiritual traditions have been saying about energy for millennia.

## Connecting to the anandamaya kosha

This is called the Bliss body because when you understand experientially that we are all one connected energy manifesting in different forms, that realization is a blissful feeling. You may have felt this sensation when you are in a state of complete absorption in what you are doing, as described by psychologist Mihaly Csikszentmihalyi in his groundbreaking book *Flow*. You experience complete connection to what you are doing, and your thoughts and the ego are no longer calling the shots. You can also experience this feeling spontaneously through meditation practices. It takes time and practice to get to that feeling, but it is achievable and, once experienced, it becomes easier to tap back into it.

You do not really "cleanse" or heal this kosha, because it is always perfect. But problems in other sheaths can cause the connection between this part of our energy body to become disconnected from the rest. You can reconnect by doing charitable works that permit you to see that the people you are helping are no different from you. Once we understand *spiritually*, rather than intellectually, that we are all one, we connect to the bliss of this kosha.

# Cleansing the protective sheath

Once you have thought about cleansing and connecting with your five koshas, you can simply maintain your energetic health by concentrating your efforts on the sum of those sheaths and visualizing it as a single protective sheath. There are several ways to cleanse this sheath. I recommend you do at least one a day and, ideally, create a monthly routine that incorporates all the suggestions below.

## SMUDGING

Burning bundles of dried herbs is a tried-and-tested way to clear not just your own aura but the aura of the space around you. This is because your senses are a great conduit to your energy body. The scent of the herbs burning helps you feel transported to a more spiritual space in which you can visualize healing your body—both physical and energetic.

You can buy ready-made smudging sticks in alternative health shops, or you can make your own with bundles of dried herbs. Just make sure you have a fireproof dish available to catch any stray embers. Light the bundle, blow it out so that the end is smoking, and pass whatever you're smudging through the fragrant smoke. You can smudge your own aura by starting at your feet and moving the smoke up the left-hand side of your body, over the top of your head and down your right-hand side. Once you've finished, make sure you extinguish the smudgestick completely.

### Herbs to smudge with:

- ✧ sage
- ✧ thyme
- ✧ rosemary
- ✧ cedar
- ✧ mugwort

## SALT BATHS

Salt has long been considered a sacred substance—the taste of our tears, our bodies, the sea and the earth. Salt is also immensely cleansing and can be used to cleanse an aura easily and quickly. Whenever you feel particularly down or tired, simply take a couple of handfuls of one of the salts below and add them to a warm bath. When sitting in the bath, visualize the saltwater sparkling with a cleansing light, and be sure to pass the water over your head and rub some of it on your belly button.

**Salts to use:**

- ✧ Epsom salt (this is not a salt in the sense of the others listed, but has many additional health benefits)
- ✧ Sea salt
- ✧ Himalayan pink salt
- ✧ Rosemary-infused salts
- ✧ Black salt (also called Kala Namak)

## CHANTING

The right sounds can be very cleansing to your aura, especially when the sounds are reverberating through your body. There are sounds connected to cleansing each chakra in the seven-chakra system (see Part 1), but there are also chants you can do that relate to a general aura cleansing without reference to a specific chakra. Try *Aah-Ummn* as a chant, opening your mouth like an O initially and then closing it and feeling the hum of the last part of the sound against your lips. Always prepare for your chant sessions by bathing, sitting in a clean room and, perhaps, lighting some incense if you like the smell of it. If you begin to feel light-headed, stop chanting, stamp your feet on the ground and rub your palms against your thighs. Chanting suits some people, but not everyone. So if you find you get headaches, earaches or feel dizzy after chanting, choose another method of aura cleansing.

## DRINK WATER

This may sound like a ridiculous suggestion, but one way in which your aura will weaken considerably is if you are not adequately hydrated. Your physical body impacts your aura, which is why certain clairvoyants can "see" illnesses in a person's aura. When you are physically healthy, you have a far greater chance of keeping your aura clear and balanced. So drink at least eight glasses of water a day and remember that you will need more on hotter days when you sweat out a lot of water.

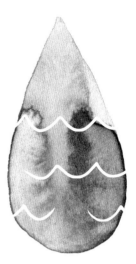

## BODY MASSAGE

One of the most enjoyable ways of clearing your aura is massage with appropriate oils. You can ask a partner or family member to give you a massage or you can massage yourself. One of the best areas to massage is your feet. This is because they connect you to the earth and are a key area for strengthening your aura. After washing them, anoint them with oil and massage from the heel up to the toes—and remember to massage between your toes as well. Be careful if you're doing this on a slippery surface, and perhaps put socks on immediately afterwards to allow the oil to sink into your feet. If you're using essential oils, make sure you use a base oil, such as almond or coconut, so that you're not applying strong oils straight onto your skin.

**Oils to use:**
- ✧ rose oil to feel loved and supported
- ✧ basil oil to attract prosperity
- ✧ lavender oil to de-stress
- ✧ rosemary oil to promote healing
- ✧ bergamot oil to energize yourself

## A CALM DEMEANOR

Try to avoid outrage, whether online or in conversation. Outrage, conflict and anger cause your aura to weaken. Dr Andrew Weil, a practitioner of integrative medicine, suggested in one of his early books on optimum health that everyone take regular "news fasts" so we don't take on negativity. This is even more useful for social media. If you don't know what the latest outrage is, you can't fall prey to its effects. Anger and counter-anger can be a very destructive cycle, and nobody—unless they have an abnormal energy exchange that I would not consider beneficial or helpful—feels better after an argument.

## WALK BAREFOOT

Connecting with the earth heals you both physically and psychically. If you can manage it, regularly walk barefoot on the earth. This is a process called "earthing," and it ensures that your body clock is calibrated to the pulse of the Earth. It connects you with your own nature and relieves you from the stress of electromagnetic waves that constantly affect our auras.

## MEDITATION

You can find a range of different meditations that you can do to work with your aura and that of others. However, a regular meditation practice, even if you're not trying to do anything in particular, is extremely beneficial. There are now several apps that can help you take a little time each day to relax. You can also take a class if you think it's too difficult to learn to meditate by yourself. Even a few moments relaxing and trying not to think about anything in particular can help you during a busy day.

# Seeing the aura

Semyon Davidovich Kirlian invented Kirlian photography in 1939, a process by which he was able to photograph the aura around living things. In 1961, Kirlian and his journalist wife, Valentina, published an article on the subject in the *Russian Journal of Scientific and Applied Photography.* Ever since that time, researchers and energy healers have used the information gained through Kirlian photography to diagnose illnesses and predict the preoccupations of the people being photographed.

The colors that appear on the photographs have been interpreted by some as corresponding to the meanings of the seven-chakra energy system, and by others as being indicative of certain personality traits and of what concerns the person has at the time of being photographed. Kirlian's work has definitely increased the interest in auras, but there was another earlier practitioner who invented a way for people to see the aura with the naked eye.

## KILNER SCREENS

Dr W.J. Kilner wrote in his 1911 book *The Human Atmosphere* about investigations he made into the human aura by virtue of his colored screens. The screens are made of thin glass with dicyanin dyes in alcohol. The operator looks through a dark screen at the light screens for a minute or so, and then looks at the person being read through a pale screen until he or she can see the aura. Regular use of the screens results in the operator eventually being able to see auras without the aid of any apparatus. Much like Magic Eye pictures, popular in student culture in the 1990s, once you have adjusted your eye to perceive the aura, it's hard to go back. A plain black or white background behind the subject is required, but looking at the aura in this way can cause pain in the eyes, so should be undertaken with care.

Theosophist Arthur E. Powell described what the aura, seen in this way, looks like in his book *The Etheric Double*: "The Inner Aura is the densest portion of the aura proper. It is usually more distinctly marked and broader in persons in robust physical health. The Outer Aura commences from the outer edge of the Inner Aura and, unlike the Inner Aura, varies in size considerably. Round the head it extends usually about 2 inches beyond the shoulders: by the sides and body of the trunk, it is a little narrower. It follows closely the contours of the body, being sometimes a little narrower down the lower limbs. Around the arms it corresponds to that encircling the legs, but is generally broader round the hands and frequently projects a long distance from the finger tips."

This last part of the description pertaining to the hands will be important for us later when we look at how to balance our auras through our hands (see pages 127–129).

## PSYCHIC SIGHT

Despite these more technical ways to see the aura, the most popular among practitioners remains the gift of psychically viewing the aura. This may not necessarily be a visual impression, and it may be that it is "viewed" through feelings and emotions that the healer gets as they sit across from you, in the influence of your aura. Some may even use the flat of the palm to "feel" the edges of the aura by placing their hand a couple of inches away from the body.

If you would like to develop such a sight, you should take care to ensure that you keep your protective sheath in top condition, as you will only be able to get clear impressions of the auras of others if your own is strong and healthy. Otherwise, you may sense gaps in their aura when it is actually a problem with your own. You can find a variety of ways to cleanse your protective sheath on pages 107-111.

# The chakras in Sufism

There are six chakras, or *lataif,* in Sufism. The Sufi chakras can be activated through trance dance or *dhikr*, Islamic devotional chanting. Different Sufi traditions attribute different colors and attributes to the energy points in the body. Some only have five points, and there are some who believe that the number of energy centers in the body is infinite since we reflect the universe within ourselves. However, all agree that the *lataif* sit mostly horizontally, across the body, rather than in the vertical formation of the more familiar seven-chakra system. Some Sufi orders do not engage in dance or music, and believe in silent rather than vocal *dhikr*.

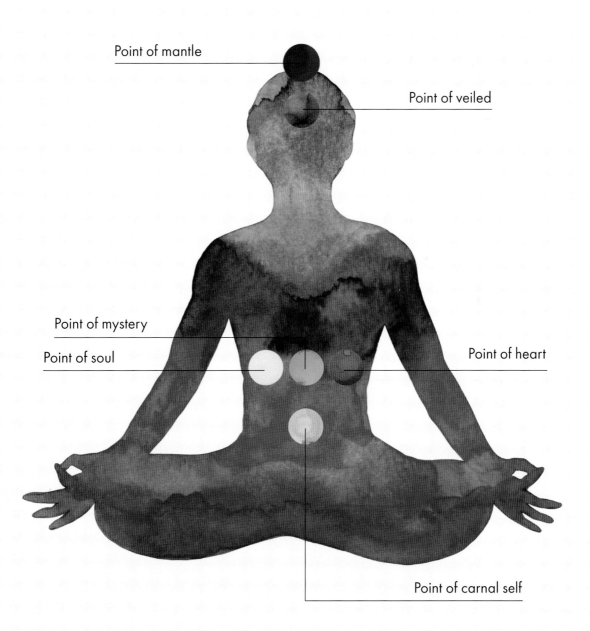

Point of mantle

Point of veiled

Point of mystery

Point of soul

Point of heart

Point of carnal self

All these differences should encourage you because, as you progress through your journey into discovering more about your own aura, you will see what feels most true to you about your energy centers. The most important thing is to trust your intuition. We are somewhat enthralled by facts, figures and science-speak in the West, but energy often uses the ethereal, the intuitive and the mysterious to bring us its best gifts. Stay alert and aware, but also trust yourself if you have a particular sense of your energy.

# Point of carnal self

- ✧ Color: **Yellow**
- ✧ Position: **Its center is in the solar plexus**

This is the chakra that pertains to the body and material existence. The body is sacred because it houses your spirit, but in order to fully move forward to the completion of your energetic destiny, you must transcend this *lataifa* (the singular term for chakra).

One of the best ways to do this is to anchor your practice in the body through *dhamal*. *Dhamal* is a Sufi trance dance, and you can obtain drumming tapes that enable you to enter into this state. It is a form of transcendence that shares much with shamanic journeying in that you lose your everyday consciousness in order to commune with the Divine. Initially, you move in rhythm to the beat, but there are no set movements; it is based purely on sensation and how the energy of the drums moves you. It is said that, once in a trance, you become a puppet with strings of energy connecting you to God, and you move whichever way your Maker wants. It is a magical way to clear your first chakra, and you will find that your body may well miraculously heal itself of any number of ailments as a result.

# Point of heart

◈ Color: **Red**
◈ Position: **Its center is an inch or so below the left breast**

Sufism is often called the ancient wisdom of the heart, so this point is an important one. It is often through the remembrance of love (and, as we saw when looking at the Anahata chakra in Part 1, true love is unconditional) that transcendence is achieved. Ultimate union with the Beloved occurs through the opening of the heart.

Having left the Point of the Carnal Self behind in your energy work, here you begin to meditate on the nature of the Divine and the fact that your soul will return to the source of all creation.

When you are in meditation, you may find that naturally, over time, you feel a warmth in your chest and a sensation of release as this *lataifa* is activated. You will feel an outpouring of love and compassion for all and, ultimately, an understanding of your true nature as a spark of divine energy made manifest for a short time only before returning home to its source.

# Point of soul

 ✧ Color: **White**
 ✧ Position: **Its center is an inch or so below the right breast**

The progression of activation of the Sufi chakras is best undertaken with a teacher. For example, chanting is based on the teachings of your tradition, and the correct chant for each *lataifa* is given to the seeker in that setting.

However, it can be revealed that many believe all *lataif* are aspects of the heart, since this is the energy center through which we gain union with the Divine. One of the ways in which you can progress from the dhamal activation of the Point of the Carnal and meditation to open the heart is to undertake gazing at this stage of your journey. There are many ways of gazing and, when you begin to see the auras of people and things, you will become very adept at gazing. Sufis use gazing at one's teacher, or into a mirror, to help unlock the truth in their hearts. You can also do so through *sagale-naseer*, the practice of gazing at the tip of one's nose. This is done when seated in meditation, having done your usual ablutions beforehand.

# Point of mystery

✧ Color: **Green**
✧ Position: **It is situated between the points of heart and soul in the middle of chest**

The nature of this *lataifa* is revealed at the correct time for the seeker. Purity is an important concept for all those who would attain the activation of this chakra. We think of purity as simply a function of cleanliness, but this does not just pertain to one's physical body or environment. You can have someone who is physically very clean residing in a tidy, immaculate place, but if they have hate in their heart, the whole energy of the person and place is polluted.

To be pure is to be kind and loving, and to remember the sacred nature of all things since we are all one. We saw earlier that your thoughts matter, so when you feel anger or irritation, stop, breathe and remember to send loving thoughts to whoever has caused you that tension. Only then will the Point of Mystery be open to you and enable you to progress on your journey to enlightenment and union with the Divine.

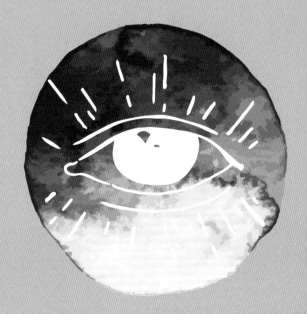

# Point of veiled

- ✧ Color: **Dark blue**
- ✧ Position: **It is situated in the middle of the forehead, popularly known as the third eye**

This is the first of the two higher *lataif*, and is the meeting point between the soul (spirit) and the body. Everything from the Divine comes to this point and is then distributed to other points. This is why whenever you see someone attaining enlightenment in the movies, their third eye is shown as being open or having a light radiating from it.

This chakra will only open and activate once the others are clear and functioning properly. This is because you must be able to handle the energies that come into your body at this stage. Often, problems occur when people are greedy for union with the Divine but they ignore the correct progression of energetic evolution. You wouldn't enter a toddler who didn't yet know how to walk properly into a marathon and expect them to complete it. In much the same way, spiritually you must learn to walk before you can run. Everything happens at the right time, so stay the course and clear your energies in preparation for when enlightenment will find you.

# Point of mantle

⋄ Color: **Shining, iridescent black**
⋄ Position: **It is situated in the crown of the head**

The mantle is a cloak that envelopes you, and this point is a center of protection. When a parent puts a loving hand on the head of a child, you get the spiritual energy of this *lataifa*. The Divine puts a hand lovingly on our heads at the Point of Mantle. We honor that loving energy by ensuring that we are a worthy recipient of it.

The responsibility we all bear for ourselves culminates at this point. Living with love in our hearts and following good energetic practices will ensure that your energy body is a pure vehicle to be crowned with this point. However, this second higher *lataifa* does not require any specific practice for its good functioning. Even if we do not activate the other *lataif*, this one is there for the protection of our eternal souls, which are not concerned with the details of our mundane existence. This can be a very cheering thought if you have problems with any of your other chakras, as nobody is ever closed off to the workings of grace.

# Physical balance

There is a strong link between your physical body and your aura. Your thoughts affect your physical body and your physical body affects your spiritual one. The three interact constantly, and good health and wellbeing rely on each aspect being well-balanced. It is always a good idea to begin with the physical, as it is the foundation upon which your energetic health is based.

# The Naaf

Naaf is a Persian word that means belly button. In the connection between the physical and the spiritual, your belly button is vitally important, and your gut is an organ to which you should pay plenty of attention. The navel is the seat of power in many occult traditions. Swami Brahmavidya wrote in *The Science of Self Knowledge* (1922): "Another great key I will give you is to be found by the contemplation of the Manipur Lotus, which is in the navel, or thereabouts. By contemplating this center, you will be able to enter and go into another person's body, take possession of that person's mind, and cause him to think and to do what you want him to do; you will obtain the power of transmuting metals, of healing the sick and afflicted, and of seership." While no moral modern person wants to take possession of another's mind, healing the sick and obtaining seership would be handy traits to have.

The word "navel" has its root in an old Anglo-Saxon word: *nafela*. The Greek word for navel is *bembix*, which literally means "whirlpool," hinting at how the movement of chakras has been described by almost all energetic medicine practitioners. Most interestingly of all, the root word for "umbilical" in Latin is *umbo*, which means the boss of a shield—the rounded, strongest part of a shield. This is a good indication of how far our strength lies in this part of our bodies.

It is not just the human body that has this center of energy; many believe there are places on Earth that serve the same function in physical geography. In Abrahamic religions, Jerusalem is considered the navel of the world. Cuzco, an important city in Peru, is named for the Quechua (Inca) word for navel. The axis mundi (or center of the Earth) is said to be the place of connection between Heaven and Earth. For the Sioux it is the Black Hills, in the Great Plains of North America. Likewise, Mount Fuji is the axis mundi of Japan.

## NAVEL-GAZING

The term "navel-gazing" is often used in a disparaging way to suggest someone who is far too interested in themselves or in a particular issue to look up and see the bigger picture. However, it actually derives from a spiritual practice common in both ancient Greek and Indian cultures. The Greeks called this *omphaloskepsis*, a contemplation of the navel that was used as an aid to meditation and communion with divinity. Yogis also undertake this practice and activate the Manipura, or solar plexus chakra, to gain insight into the nature of the Universe. This chakra center has, in the Western alternative spiritual tradition, been associated with power and purpose. It is considered the seat of will.

You should protect this power center through practical techniques such as rubbing salt over your belly button when having energy-cleansing baths, or wearing a peace silk belt around your waist, under your clothes. Most important of all, keep your gut in good health by following a nutritious diet and paying attention to the foods and drinks that disagree with your digestive system.

# Yoga practice

Often there is an assumption that you need to attend classes, buy expensive yoga clothes, mats, blocks and all manner of other equipment in order to practice *asanas*. The truth is that, while yoga classes are useful for ensuring you are doing the postures correctly, you can learn yoga easily. Many people have a daily practice based on watching videos online, while others practice from books. All you really need is comfortable clothing that you can move freely in, and a non-slip, comfortable surface to practice on—this doesn't need to be a yoga mat; you could just use an ordinary rug if it is non-slip. Yoga is always practiced in bare feet.

A morning yoga practice feels very different from an evening one. Begin with 10 minutes each morning and build your practice from that.

Don't practice on a full stomach, and make sure you are sufficiently hydrated. It is good to begin alternate-nostril breathing, as this balances your body and builds a beginning to your *asanas* or postures. On the following pages, there are some simple practices that can help the cleansing of your chakras or the healing of your aura. You can use them in conjunction with the postures given in Part 1, or as the core of a regular yoga practice.

# Alternate-Nostril Breathing

1  Sit cross-legged on the floor, with your back upright. You can use a pillow or cushion to support you if you need it. If you find it hard to sit on the floor, you can sit on a chair. Just be sure to place your feet flat on the ground, hip-width apart.

2  Close your eyes if you feel comfortable doing so. If not, you can leave them shuttered slightly, maintaining a soft gaze.

3  Put your left hand gently on your lap, palm up.

4  Exhale completely and bring the thumb of your right hand up to your right nostril to close it.

5  Inhale through your left nostril and then block it with your little and ring fingers; release your right nostril and exhale out of it.

6  You can rest your index and middle fingers on the third eye.

7  Inhale through the right nostril and close it again with your thumb. Release your left nostril and exhale out of it. This is now one full cycle of alternate-nostril breathing.

8  You can do this for about five minutes or for a number of cycles, but always finish a complete cycle.

This breathing exercise, called *nadi shodhana pranayama,* is a powerful way to balance your energies and focus your mind. It helps with anxiety, lowers stress, and helps your respiratory and cardiovascular systems. It promotes overall wellbeing and is a good daily practice to maintain. However, you should not practice this if you have a cold. And if you have asthma, a lung issue, or any other ailment that affects your breathing, speak to your doctor before you do this exercise.

## Prevention, not cure

Yoga is based on the principle that you should prevent illness through a regular practice rather than cure yourself when you are sick. Alla Svirinskaya is a fifth-generation energy healer from Russia who champions sustainable wellness. She says, "It is about wellness as a necessity. Like taking a shower or brushing your teeth. This is a necessity. It is also your necessity to be well. It's not a luxurious aspiration.

"Often, people discover spirituality or go to their doctors or healers when they're at breaking point. Only then, they do something. They're clearing their energy and doing energy rebalancing when they're completely overwhelmed and feel very toxic within. I don't want energy work and energy clearing to be as a desperate SOS kind of measure. What I'm trying to achieve is that people start looking at prophylactics for prevention as part of their daily routine."

Alla makes an excellent point. Ideally, we should not be clearing and balancing our auras once we are already sick: good energetic health should be a daily concern.

# Hand healing

One of the best ways you can balance your aura is through your hands. The aura is denser here, so your hands should be more naturally protected than other parts of your body. Hands are also connected to all the organs and energy points in your body, so manipulating your hands can help you heal that part of your body and your life.

However, you can also impart healing through hands-on touch. We have already seen the beneficial effects of massage, but once you are able to view the aura, you will also be able to direct energy through your hands to balance and heal the other person's aura.

You can visualize opening your hands' chakras by shaking them gently in front of you with the palms facing toward you. You can also do so by rubbing your hands vigorously together until they feel warm and tingly. That sensation is an indication that you have activated the chakras of your hands and can apply them to draw energy from the universal source into whoever you are healing.

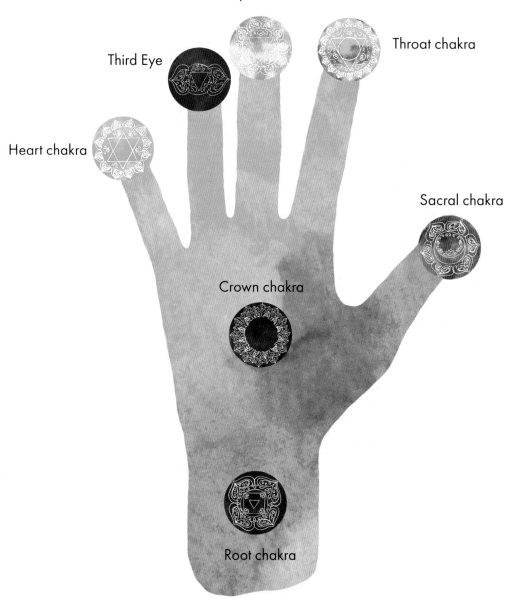

Solar plexus chakra

Third Eye

Throat chakra

Heart chakra

Sacral chakra

Crown chakra

Root chakra

## HENNA CIRCLES

A simple henna design, such as the one shown, is often used in the subcontinent to cool the hands (and consequently the hand chakras) as well as to attract prosperity and good luck to the wearer. Henna is a natural dye that has been used around the world in rites and rituals.

# Energy sphere

One of the ways you can both sense and
balance your aura is to do the following exercise.

1   Sit in a straight-backed chair with your feet flat on the floor.

2   Hold your hands out in front of you with the palms facing
    inwards.

3   Draw your hands in until they are an inch apart, but not
    touching.

4   Feel the sensation of resistance between your palms. This is
    your aura's energy that you're feeling.

5   Move your hands apart and together again until you get a
    clearer sensation of the energy between them.

6   You can then visualize that energy forming a sphere that you
    are holding in your hands like a ball.

7   Within that ball of light, visualize your entire body with a
    strong, healthy aura around it.

8   Finally, send that energetic sphere up to the heavens above
    your head.

# Your sacred space

Have you ever been in the midst of a city crowd? Most of us feel very uncomfortable in such a situation. This is because there are several auras chaotically assaulting the borders of our own aura. On occasion, if your own aura is weak, you will attract people and situations that cause irritation and frustration in daily life. A delayed train. An impatient commuter shoving you out of the way. Spilt coffee.

The way to prevent this from happening is to ensure that you are recharging somewhere that is completely in alignment with your energy body. Your home may not currently be a sacred space in the way that a church or temple might be, but you should aim to get it there. You can create a sacred space more or less anywhere, but there are certain things you should do when you're first starting to clear your space.

## DECLUTTER AND DETOX

While it's fine to have a lot of possessions or collections, clutter is not good for your aura or the auras of the people and animals that live in your home. Clutter can be defined as something you don't need and don't love. People often harm their auras by not handling their clutter. This is because clutter essentially represents decisions that haven't been made. So every time you see that stack of papers that hasn't been filed, or that pile of clothes that hasn't been donated or washed, you feel guilt. Guilt is toxic to your aura. Prolonged guilt will damage your aura, so you must address it as soon as possible.

Having cleared your clutter (and get help if you find it too stressful to deal with by yourself), you should give everything in your home a spring clean. Do not use harsh chemicals, as they inevitably hurt both your physical body and your auric one. There are many natural ingredients, including baking soda, lemon and vinegar, that are good for cleaning; also, there are plenty of health-food stores that stock natural, chemical-free household cleaners.

Once this is done, you'll find that the energy has shifted somewhat in your home. At this point, you can dedicate it to your highest good by smudging (see page 108) and stating your intention to create a nourishing, safe and happy home.

Then, walk from your front door clockwise around each room in your house, holding your hands out in front of you. Try to sense the energy of your furniture, possessions, décor and layout. Does anything feel a bit "sticky," or as if it's in the wrong place? Now is a good time to rearrange furniture or thin out artwork if it doesn't feel right.

## COLORS AND THEMES

Blues are among the most calming and aura-friendly colors to have in your home. White is also very soothing. However, do not reject reds and oranges automatically, as a deep red bedroom can be reminiscent of the womb and can therefore feel very safe and cozy. Orange is also great for kitchens, as it stimulates the appetite and aids digestion.

Choose patterns, motifs and themes with care, as each has meaning and consequences for how you will feel in your space. Generally, materials such as wood and textiles are better for the human aura than metal and plastic, so try to make sure that pieces of furniture, such as your bed, are made of wood.

Share your space with plants and animals, if you can. Ferns and spider plants are great air purifiers, and have calming auras that will ensure the overall atmosphere in your house remains clean and uplifting.

Pets are excellent at reading auras, and will naturally gravitate toward those whose auras indicate that they are friendly and good. They also sense when you need a cuddle due to emotional distress, and will attempt to cheer you up without prompting.

## DIGITAL DETOX

It is not practical to recommend that you do away with all digital devices, since most of our lives are now lived on apps and mobile phones. However, you should put away your phone when doing two vital things: sleeping and eating. The electromagnetism that mobile phones emit when in use affect our auras badly. It is simple enough to leave your phone charging in a different room when you go to bed. You should also put down the phone and turn off the TV when you're eating. You can help this process by having a dining table or a dedicated place where you sit to eat. Make meals sacrosanct, and always give your full attention to the process of nourishing your body.

When items like TVs, computers and stereos are not in use, turn them off at the socket rather than leaving them on sleep. This is to ensure that any electromagnetic frequencies are kept to a minimum in your home. If you want to get really radical in the pursuit of a clear aura, consider not having a TV at all. I know a number of very happy people who don't have one.

# Places of power

There are some people who return again and again to the same vacation destination each year. They visit the same bars and restaurants, see the same sights, and enjoy the same activities at around the same time each year. You may consider them unadventurous, but actually they are very fortunate for, generally speaking, these are people who have found the aura of a place that agrees with their own personal energy makeup.

If you manage to find a place that attracts you and makes you feel great, it may well be your own personal place of power. You feel invigorated there; your shoulders relax, as does your jaw, and you feel as though you have been transported to a delightful place.

## FINDING YOUR PLACE IN THE WORLD

There are some obvious contenders for finding a place to give you solace. Stone circles have traditionally been centers of energy and ritual for Pagan and Neolithic communities in Britain and Ireland. These are powerful, not just because of where they're located (usually built along energetic lines that are particularly potent), but also because the aura of a place is influenced by its history. Where sacred rituals and rites have taken place, the area takes on an aura of power and transcendence that is almost magical. This is, on occasion, ruined by human beings when they commodify the experience and turn it into a gimmick or a novelty, but you can still find amazing places off the beaten track that align to the cravings of our auras.

Water is another attraction for the human aura. Oceanfront and riverside properties always cost more money because of the truism that we are attracted to water. Moving water will keep the energy of a place clear and light, while stagnant water in ponds or manmade lakes can exude melancholy due to the lack of connection with the world's water system.

However, not all manmade structures suffer from this problem. Wells and portals or holes made in stone act as energy points from which you can draw energy into the world. In myth and legend, we often hear of these holes, and know to fear and respect their power. Passing through a stone circle almost always leads you to the fairy world, so these gateways have a touch of the magical to them.

If you find a place of power that resonates with you, but you are unable to visit it as often as you like, you can connect with it using meditation by visualizing it. This is a great way to enhance your auric connection to the area, and you may find that opportunities begin to open up that will lead you to being able to visit it in real life soon.

If you find that you are living in a part of the world that doesn't agree with you or your aura, you will never be able to find happiness until you leave, so you must work to bring about that change. This can't be done by criticizing or denigrating the place where you live. It can only be done by praising the place where you think you will be happier. Attraction rather than rejection must be your operating procedure.

# Helping others

Healing your friends and family is an act that not only helps them, but also helps you. This is because if you could see your aura, you would see tendrils of energy stretching out and connecting you with everyone you know. Some tendrils, for example those connecting you to your life partner, are like thick cords that connect you strongly to another person's energy. Others, like those connecting you to the cashier at your local supermarket, are faint but nevertheless present. Whenever we think about someone, a tendril zooms out and connects with their energy. It doesn't matter how physically far away that person is—the tendril will still find them. Some religions believe that when you pray for your dead, the prayer energy reaches the person in heaven and gives them both pleasure and merit.

## TEA AND SYMPATHY

While not every person you love will want to explore the world of auras with you, you can help heal their aura by doing something quite mundane. Sharing tea with someone is an easy way to connect with their energy, give them some of your healing vibes, and make them feel loved.

**These teas are particularly good for the aura:**

- ✧ Chamomile
- ✧ Rosehip
- ✧ Nettle
- ✧ Peppermint
- ✧ Jasmine

## AFFIRMATIONS

If you have a friend who is a little more open-minded about auric healing, you can try partnered affirmations. An affirmation is a positive, present-timed statement of what you would like to manifest in your life. When you say them aloud with a friend who repeats them back to you, it creates an auric bond that makes the outcome far more likely. This is because there is someone else witnessing your affirmation and confirming it back to you.

So you might say, "I am strong and healthy." Then your friend says to you, "You are strong and healthy."

Or you might do an affirmation to manifest wealth or a loving relationship. What you choose to affirm is up to you, but the statement must be in the present tense, so no "I will be…". And it must be positive, so no statements that begin "I am not…"

After you say your affirmations to each other and repeat them back to each other, make a note of what you said and the date when you said it; then look back once your outcomes have manifested. Did anything not manifest? What do you or your friend believe is blocking that outcome for you both? How can you convince yourself?

For example, suppose you affirmed "I am fit enough to run a marathon," but you didn't manage to run one despite your friend affirming it back to you. It may be that you are fit enough to run a marathon, but you didn't affirm that you have successfully completed a marathon. Or it may be that you have done nothing beyond the affirmation to meet your goal. The affirmation will help, but you still need to put in the training sessions. Reaffirm your goal and report back to your friend each time you undertake a training session so that your friend is also convinced that your goal will be met.

Interestingly, Alla Svirinskaya, the hugely talented Russian medical doctor and healer mentioned earlier, has discovered that it is best to say affirmations in the language you used from when you learned to talk until around the age of 10. For me this is Punjabi and, in learning this nugget of useful information, I found my affirmations moved up a level as a result of saying them in Punjabi.

## ABSENCE OF AN AURA

In your early days of trying to see auras, you may find that you do not see anything at all—and that is absolutely fine. However, some say that the absence of an aura can be a sign of impending death. The famous psychic Edgar Cayce wrote of a very sad and dramatic experience in his pamphlet *Auras*. He had been shopping in a department store and was going to take the elevator. As the doors opened, he felt a dark hollowness inside it, despite it being quite full of people. At that exact moment, a red sweater caught his eye, and he motioned for the elevator to leave without him, intending to catch the next one. The cable snapped on the elevator and all the occupants plunged to their deaths. Cayce wrote how odd the whole experience had been, since he didn't even like the color red. Thankfully, in our explorations of auras, not seeing an aura does not mean anything other than that we need a lot more practice.

part 3

HERBALISM

# Basic Herbal Preparations

The following recipes are ideal for home use and self-care. However, professional herbalists in clinical settings (and retail product craft makers) are encouraged to follow far more precise scientific calculations, alchemy, measurements and ratios in their practice, to get the most health benefits and potency out of their products. For that, I cannot recommend Richo Cech's book, *Making Plant Medicine*, enough. But, for the home health needs of just about anyone else, these basic recipes will do just fine.

Home herbalism, or cottage herbalism (or kitchen-witchin', as I like to call it), has been around for so long that I could hardly call the following how-to's anything close to a recipe, let alone a *signature* recipe: they are just one way to do things.

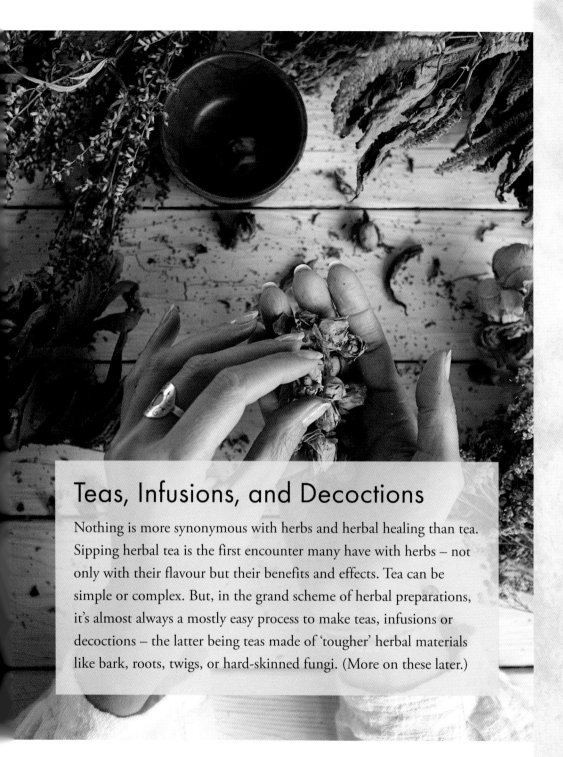

# Teas, Infusions, and Decoctions

Nothing is more synonymous with herbs and herbal healing than tea. Sipping herbal tea is the first encounter many have with herbs – not only with their flavour but their benefits and effects. Tea can be simple or complex. But, in the grand scheme of herbal preparations, it's almost always a mostly easy process to make teas, infusions or decoctions – the latter being teas made of 'tougher' herbal materials like bark, roots, twigs, or hard-skinned fungi. (More on these later.)

# Simple Tea Recipe

While it's true that you can make tea out of any herb, a simple tea brings out the best in fresh, leafy herbs, fruits or flowers, especially a botanical's flavours and fragile constituents. That said, there's no reason not to enjoy a quick tea of herbal roots, bark and the like. These won't be nearly as potent or, in some cases, as flavourful as a decoction, but that doesn't mean they're not enjoyable or healthy.

**STEP 1** – Bring water to a boil.

**STEP 2** – In the meantime, ready a mug or teapot with the tea amounts you wish to use. Most herbs make an excellent tea when you use 1–3 tablespoons (approx. 2g to 6g) of herbal material per cup measurement, or average mug size full of hot water. (Obviously, make sure to boil and prepare ample water.)

Herbal material can be either measured teabag amounts (store-bought or handmade) or placed into an infuser in your vessel of choice.

**STEP 3** – Pour boiled water over tea in your teacup, mug, pot, infuser or other vessel. Let it steep for at least 5 minutes. Sip and enjoy while still hot, and flavour lightly with lemon juice, honey or any other flavourful or health-boosting addition you like, and experience the benefits. **Make as many cups as needed until the desired effect is achieved, or enjoy 1-2 cups daily for long-term nutritive benefits (first, be sure to check 'Warnings Before Use' with any herb you make tea from in this book).**

# Herbal Infusion (or Compress)

All teas are infusions; they're one and the same. In my own personal practice, however, I tend to label infusions as stronger herbal teas, with more specific medicinal purposes owing to their stronger nature, of course. Infusions don't always need to be taken internally. If you want to make a herbal compress (for topical use, such as minor burns or wounds), prepare an infusion. A compress, or wash (for wounds), can be used for superficial cuts, skin issues and the like.

Or, like a tea, you can simply sip an infusion for a stronger bout of effects than from regular herbal tea. Most herbalists also tend to make higher amounts of infusions: either for multiple compresses, or for drinking regularly over several days (refrigerating and/or re-boiling it, of course).

**STEP 1** – Bring water to a boil.

**STEP 2** – In the meantime, ready a large teapot or other stovetop pot with the infusion amounts you wish to use. These will be a higher ratio than teas. My personal ratio for a very strong tea infusion is ½–1 cup herb (dried or fresh) per 3.8 litres of water.

**STEP 3** – Obviously, a teabag or infuser is not going to cut it for a strong infusion made in plentiful amounts (though large infusers can and do exist). I place all raw herbal material straight into the pot of boiling water, stir it in, and turn off the heat.

**STEP 4** – Let the infusion steep for at least 10 minutes – some herbalists say at least 30 minutes, but there are no hard-and-fast rules. For a very potent brew, turn the pot on low instead of completely off, letting the herbs infuse for another hour.

**STEP 5** – Once it reaches the desired strength, pour the infusion through a strainer into yet another clean stovetop pot to remove the herbal material. Pour into a cup (or multiple cups) as needed; flavour, sip and enjoy. **Make as many cups as needed until the desired effect is achieved, or enjoy 1–2 cups daily for long-term nutritive benefits (first, be sure to check 'Warnings Before Use' with any herb you make tea from in this book).**

You may also leave an infusion on low heat to enjoy multiple cups. Or turn off the heat, refrigerate, then reheat and enjoy later (ideally, infusions should be reheated and consumed within a week).

*For using as a compress or wash,* let the infusion cool. Then, using a clean cloth, apply the liquid to the area as many times as needed, or until the infusion is gone.

# Decoctions

Decoctions are reserved for the toughest herbal ingredients such as roots, bark, twigs and resilient fungi (e.g. reishi mushrooms, which are not explored in this book). The herbal materials don't steep. Instead, they are boiled for a long period of time, sometimes with water replenished or replaced as levels get lower. Like infusions, decoctions can be used for topical purposes in the form of a compress, too.

**STEP 1** – Bring water to a boil in a large stovetop pot.

**STEP 2** – Unlike teas or infusions, decoctions are made by putting the herbal material straight into the boiling water. I use the same ratio for decoctions as with infusions (roughly ½–1 cup herb per 3.8 litres of water). Place the herbal material in the pot, either before the water comes to a boil or as soon as it starts to boil.

**STEP 3** – Turn the boil down to a simmer, and let the herb infuse for between 1 and 2 hours. This helps extract constituents from the tougher herbal ingredients. One hour should produce a good decoction – however, you can decoct for much longer, and some herbalists even let it warm overnight, like a stew (ensuring that there is enough water, of course!).

**STEP 4** – However long you choose to decoct, always make sure to stay nearby and keep an eye on the process. If the water begins to get low – or at a level lower than the herbal matter – add more, and let it continue to simmer. This is especially crucial if you decide to make a decoction overnight.

**STEP 5** – Once it is to your liking, pour the decoction through a strainer into yet another clean stovetop pot or stainless-steel bowl, to remove the herbal material. Pour into a cup (or multiple cups) as needed; flavour, sip and enjoy. **Make as many cups as needed until the desired effect is achieved, or enjoy 1–2 cups daily for long-term nutritive benefits (first, be sure to check 'Warnings Before Use' with any herb you make tea from in this book).**

As with an infusion, you can keep a decoction on a low heat to enjoy multiple cups. Or turn off the heat, refrigerate, then reheat and enjoy later (like infusions, decoctions should be consumed within a week).

*For using as a compress,* let the decoction cool. Then, using a clean cloth, apply the liquid to the area as many times as needed, or until the decoction is gone.

# Infused Oils

Why make an infused oil? There are a couple of reasons. Before making a salve, you will need to make an infused oil. But not all infused oils necessarily need to be made into salves. Oils can also be used on their own, topically, just like salves for healing purposes; they can also be delightful when used in the kitchen – garlic-infused oil comes to mind (though less so for a topical salve).

Infused oils can be made with either fresh or dried herbs, a single herb or a combination of herbs. **Some herbalists follow tight ratios of herbs to oil, but generally, one part herbal matter to three parts oil is a good balance, and has worked for me**. Fresh infusions are favoured for salve-making, while dried herbs are preferable for culinary infused oils. This is because fresh herbs can impart water into the oil and increase the risk of pathogenic contamination if taken internally – which is why it is best to conserve these for topical use only.

There are both crude and sophisticated ways to make infused oils, and the more sophisticated ways take more time, money and tools than a beginning herbalist may possess. Fortunately, the basic ways of creating herb-infused oils (not essential oils, to be clear – these require distillation) are nearly as good for home use.

**Note on proper oils:** If you have standards of health and purity for the oils you buy for cooking, you'll want to have the same for your herb-infused oils. Be sure to purchase chemical-free, unrefined and otherwise pure choices.

## SUN-INFUSED OIL

**STEP 1** – Place a measurement of herbs (single or multiple) in a clean jar that can be shut with an airtight lid (a standard large canning jar works great).

**STEP 2** – Pour oil over the herbs in the jar. Make sure they are completely covered – this will ensure a good infusion.

**STEP 3** – Place the jar in a sunny spot (such as a windowsill) to absorb a good amount of heat from the sun daily. South-facing windows are best since they'll ensure the best exposure and warmth – and it's important to make sure the container is tightly closed.

**STEP 4** – Let the oil infuse in this way for about a week. Feel free to check on it and stir the mixture occasionally.

**STEP 5** – After the week is over, strain the oil with a fine strainer or piece of cheesecloth into another container (you may use an empty, cleaned cooking-oil bottle; be sure to label it). Store in a cool, dry place and make sure the bottle or container is as airtight as possible.

**For internal use, take 1–2 tbsp. (or standard spoonfuls) as needed for benefits – or combine with vinegar and add to fresh greens or salads. Apply to unbroken skin for topical benefits, depending on the herb (see monographs).**

## DOUBLE BOILER INFUSED OIL

Why use a double boiler? Oils can be volatile (and smoky) when overheated. Even if left unattended only briefly, an unsupervised stovetop-infused oil could reach a boil or simmer quite quickly. Not only would this ruin the final product, it could pose a fire hazard, as oils can catch fire if they become too hot.

When going this route, purchase a good oil with a high smoke point. (Be careful not to exceed the smoke point: check the oil temperature regularly with a clean meat thermometer.) Smoking oil can pose a fire hazard, of course, but it can also destroy any health properties and nutrients in the herbs.

Personal favourites for the double boiler infused oil are sunflower seed oil, avocado oil, almond oil, olive oil, jojoba and coconut oil – the latter two are wonderful for skin-nourishment salves, especially accompanied by aloe. Again, some of these have lower smoke points and will therefore require a more watchful eye to avoid burning. You can either use a proper double boiler, or fashion a rudimentary one, which is explained in the following steps.

**STEP 1** – Place a measurement of herbs in a clean stovetop pot (preferably stainless steel) and pour oil over the herbs. If using a double boiler, place the herbs and oil in the top chamber.

**STEP 2** – In a separate stovetop pot (with a copper bottom), place a good level of water for a consistent boil of 1–2 hours. (If using a double boiler, add this water to the bottom chamber.) Obviously, the higher the volume of herbs and oil you plan on infusing, the higher the volume of water should be. (As a general rule, equal parts of water and oil work well.)

**STEP 3** – Place the double boiler setup on the stove and bring the water in the lower pot to a boil with the oil- and herb-filled pot set on top. Once it reaches a boil, turn down the heat slightly, to a strong simmer.

**STEP 4** – Let the oil simmer for at least 1 to 2 hours. You are free to infuse it longer, if desired. If the oil changes color, you'll know that it has begun to take on the compounds in the infusing herbs (most, but not all, oils will change color in response to taking on herbal compounds).

**STEP 5** – Once satisfied with the infusion, turn down the heat and let cool. Once cooled to a lukewarm temperature, strain the oil with a fine strainer or piece of cheese-cloth into another container (you may use an empty, cleaned cooking-oil bottle; be sure to label it).

**STEP 6** – Store in a cool, dry place and make sure the bottle or container is as airtight as possible. **For internal use, take 1–2 tbsp. (or standard spoonfuls) as needed for benefits – or combine with vinegar and add to fresh greens or salads. Apply to unbroken skin for topical benefits, depending on the herb (see Monographs).**

# Basic Salve

Any infused oil can be transformed into a salve or balm with the addition of beeswax. Salves are perfect for joint, muscle and skin issues (but not so much for wounds) including arthritis, muscle cramps or sunburn when rubbed into the skin, with the help of herbs like arnica, comfrey and others. Balms, of course, can be rubbed on the lips and are perfect for moistening and emollient herbs such as aloe or plantain (be sure to check out the Herbal Monographs section for more information on these).

There are differing opinions among herbalists on the perfect ratio of beeswax to oil. **I tend to take one quarter (¼) of the volume of the oil, and convert that into a solid measurement for adding into the oil (grams or solid ounces).** The same concerns about purity and sustainability of oil apply to beeswax. Make sure you're getting a pure product that is chemical- and additive-free; buying from a local beekeeper is ideal if you want to have the best quality and integrity in your salve or balm.

**The steps for salve-making are simple, and preceded by the creation of either a sun-infused oil or a double boiler oil – your choice.** However, if you want to make a salve in one night, or whip one up as quickly as possible, use the double boiler method and not the sun-infused one.

That said, you can still create a salve from sun-infused oil; the directions will just vary (see the following steps). In either case, make sure you have your salve jars ready before you start – these should be shallow containers into which you'll be pouring your salves to cool. For home use, I love using very small Mason jars (or Kilner jars in the UK).

**First, for creating a salve, simply follow your preferred infused-oil directions.** Then:

**STEP 1** – While your infused oil is still hot during the creation process (and the heat is turned off), drop in your measurement of beeswax and let it dissolve in the hot oil in your double boiler.

If you are making a sun-infused oil into a salve, you can take your final product here and place it in the top chamber of your double boiler. Bring it up to a heat level that will melt the beeswax, then add your wax (again, while the heat is turned off).

**STEP 2** – While still hot, stir the oil with a stainless-steel spoon to make sure the wax is fully incorporated – but only do this briefly. While the oil and beeswax mixture is still quite hot, pour into your salve jars. If you're after a particular salve 'consistency', you have the option of letting the mixture cool in the pot (you'll find out why in the next step).

**STEP 3** – Once fully cooled in the jars (if you choose this option), your salves are ready. But, if you (like me) are picky about your salve's consistency, the process doesn't have to end here.

Depending on the oil and herbs you use – especially if you're using fresh herbs, which can add water to the final product – even the most well-measured oil-to-wax ratio can bring you an undesirable salve consistency. It can sometimes be on the runny side, no matter how closely you follow directions.

**Checking and correcting salve consistency:** To find out if the consistency meets your requirements (and correct it), test the mixture with a spoon and rub it into your fingers. Scrape some off the top of your cooled mixture (if you left it to cool in the double boiler); if it cooled in the jars, take some from there (although it may ruin that nice, smooth final 'lip balm' appearance).

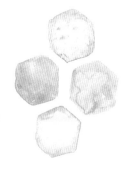

**My favourite way to salve consistency:** there is almost always some residue from the salve in the double boiler, even if you poured it off into your jars. However, here's the advantage of simply letting it cool in the double boiler: if it's not quite the right consistency, you can just get the burner going and heat it up again.

With the jars, you'll have to scoop your salve back into the double boiler again (unless you're pretty confident of the consistency). My method will save you time and mess.

**Too runny?** Add more beeswax, and melt it in. **Not soft enough?** Add a bit more oil, which will dilute the final product, but still render it useful. After this, let the salve cool again in your preferred way, check the consistency again, and repeat as many times as necessary until you get the consistency you like.

Once complete, apply salve topically as needed onto unbroken skin (or superficial wounds or burns, if using a wound or burn healer like aloe or pine).

# Poultice

Using herbs topically doesn't require an elaborate recipe. Poultices are a perfect example of this; they are typically whipped up on the spot for topical use and are very effective (and safe) for non-serious superficial cuts, wounds, burns, bug bites, or anything that could be infected. They are also appropriate for other topical uses.

**A poultice is basically a crushed-up mixture or plaster of herbs, preferably fresh (some of them are quite 'sensational', to say the least).** Some great gentle poultice candidates are comfrey, arnica, and plantain. Other 'intense' herbs like mustard seed, peppermint and even cayenne pepper or garlic have therapeutic effects as poultices, but can be too intense for some.

That said, if it's something you wish to try (considering the caustic cautions) your poultice could have some aloe gel or other soothing compound for the skin added to lessen uncomfortable chemical reactions. It's a fair price to pay for a proper poultice, one of the oldest and most powerful herbal preparation remedies.

**STEP 1** – Gather the fresh herbs or spices you plan to use. Also gather any 'binders' or other ingredients you may wish to add to your poultice for additional effects: some use flour, corn meal (polenta), cooking oil or a bit of aloe gel to make it into a soothing paste, or to allow the poultice to stick to the skin (keep in mind skin allergens, of course – especially to flour, wheat and gluten). However, binders aren't essential.

**STEP 2** – Using your preferred method, grind your herbs. You may use a culinary coffee grinder, food processor, blender or cheese grater (with herbal roots such as comfrey). Or do it the old-fashioned way, by hand with a mortar and pestle. Grind your additives or binders in with these. Regardless, make sure you use clean tools.

Fresh herbs can also be simply chopped up or finely minced with a well-sharpened chef's knife.

**STEP 3** – Apply the poultice to the affected area. Keep in mind (and prepare yourself for) any chemical reaction that may occur with more caustic herbs on wounds, burns etc. (such as mint or mustard). Avoid this type of application altogether if you're uncertain of your pain tolerance.

For respiratory issues, or to ease breathing, apply poultices to the chest or neck, so they can be inhaled and open up your air passages (think of a vapour rub here). Poultices are also popular for intramuscular pain or to speed the healing of bones and ligaments without broken skin (arnica and comfrey come to mind for this). Once the desired effect is achieved, rinse away herbal matter and cleanse skin.

# Syrups

The herbal cough syrup has a long place and history in the herbalism world – and obviously a sweet spot, too. One of the most favoured (and flavoured) vehicles for respiratory herbs, syrups can also be made for enjoyment first and natural healing second – not just for soothing coughs or sore throats, but also for flavouring teas, cocktails and foods.

The best part? You're already more than halfway to a syrup when you create a strong infusion or decoction. The rest is easy. I've worked with many different ratios and have done a lot of eyeballing over the years when making my syrups, which happen to be one of my favourite preparations. One part honey to two parts water for syrup has generally worked out for me, although three parts water has worked as well. However, much like other herbal preparations (I'm thinking of herbal salves here), I adjust herbal syrups for consistency at the very end.

**STEP 1** – Refer to the sections above on either infusions or decoctions to get your herbal syrup going – your choice will depend on the herb (or herbs) you wish to use.

The syrup-making process begins when the herbs are fully filtered or strained out of the final infusion or decoction product and placed back into a large enough stovetop pot (preferably with a copper bottom) and ready to reheat on the stove.

**STEP 2** – Measure your honey (using a roughly 1:2 honey to water ratio) and add to the stovetop pot. Bring all of this to a boil. Once a boil is reached, turn it down to medium-low, or a strong but low simmer.

**STEP 3** – Simmering time for your syrup can vary, but usually lasts 1 hour, sometimes up to 2 hours (depending, of course, on the volume of syrup you are making). Either way, if you're making a syrup, it is something to stick around for and watch, to make sure it does not overboil.

As it simmers, you can also check the consistency of your syrup with a stainless-steel spoon (wait for it to cool and give it a taste for mouthfeel, thickness, etc.). Once it reaches your desired consistency, it is finished – it could be a more watery or runny syrup, or thicker in consistency, your choice, though you obviously don't want a syrup that's *too* runny.

You also have the option of boiling the mixture all the way down for the thickest syrup possible. You'll know the mixture cannot be boiled down any thicker when the syrup begins to actively 'foam', rising up to the edge of the stovetop pot. At this point, be sure to turn off the heat and remove it from the burner immediately, before it overflows. (This is why it's wise to stay close and keep an eye on your syrup.)

**STEP 4** – Let the syrup cool down completely. Store in clean jars or bottles that close tightly, and keep it refrigerated. Unlike pure honey, herbal syrups are not shelf-stable, as they may contain water harbouring microbes (usually mould) that may grow on the top layer of your syrup.

Use your syrups within 6 to 12 months. **Take 1–2 tbsp. (or standard spoonfuls) as needed for benefits (first, be sure to check 'Warnings Before Use' with any herb you make syrup from in this book).** As you use them, you may start to notice their flavour waning, so use them quickly – it's a sign that their wellness benefits could be slipping away too. Herbs in this book that make pleasant-tasting syrups are lemon balm, angelica, white pine, sumac and even agrimony. These herbal syrups can also improve the flavour of less palatable remedies, such as valerian root or lion's mane.

# Vinegars and Shrubs

In the same vein as syrups, vinegars and preparations made with them hold a special place in the herbal world (and in my heart). No medium is better at extracting and preserving vitamins and minerals – and much can be done to make them flavourful, enjoyable and unique, in addition to remedial.

Herbs known to be nutrient dense, like stinging nettle, lion's mane and other medicinal mushrooms (shiitake, reishi etc.) are fantastic candidates for herbal vinegars. Obviously, your favourite culinary seasoning herbs – garlic, rosemary, sage and the like – can make for intriguing vinegars for both food and wellness use. Sour or 'piney' flavoured herbs (juniper, pine, rhubarb or sumac) can have the best brought out in them flavour-wise with the help of a simple, light vinegar – and their properties are preserved too.

Opt for vinegars that are pure, light and have no other ingredients, such as white vinegar or rice vinegar (avoid balsamic or flavoured vinegar). Apple cider vinegar is one of my favourites if you want to add a touch of fermentation, and you get all the health benefits of ACV mixed into your creation, too.

Vinegars are straight-forward preparations. I personally do not follow a ratio for creating a herbal vinegar. I simply fill up the entire container I plan to use with my preferred herbs.

# SIMPLE VINEGAR

**STEP 1** – Take a clean, closeable container (a Mason/Kilner jar works well) and fill it with a herb or combination of herbs.

**STEP 2** – Cover the herbs with the vinegar of your choice and seal it tightly. Keep in mind: if you're using steel or any type of metal lid, place a section of greaseproof paper, baking parchment or even newspaper in between the mouth of the jar and the lid. This protects the metal from being oxidized by the vinegar, which can cause the lid to rust and foul up your vinegar.

**STEP 3** – Shake the jar vigorously when closed, then refrigerate for a week to infuse. If you're using apple cider vinegar and would like a touch of fermentation in the mix (not much – only a subtle raise in probiotic acetic acid bacteria), leave it to infuse at room temperature for 24 hours, then refrigerate.

**STEP 4** – Over the course of the week, whenever you think of it, give the jar a shake. This will help release more herbal compounds and flavours (and it's a nice bicep workout, honestly).

**STEP 5** – After the week is over, put the vinegar through a fine strainer to remove all herbal matter. Bottle the final product in a glass jar or bottle. Don't forget to create a barrier between the mouths of your containers and any metal lids to prevent oxidation and spoilage.

Store your vinegar in the fridge. For short periods of time, it can be kept at room temperature in a dark, dry place. I recommend using the vinegar within 6 to 12 months. **Take 1–2 tbsp. (or standard spoonfuls) of vinegar internally as needed, or mix into greens or salads. (First, be sure to check 'Warnings Before Use' with any herb you make vinegar from in this book.)**

# Tinctures, Extracts and Bitters

Herbalists consider tinctures (alcohol-preserved preparations of herbs) the ultimate herbal creation, and one of the best ways to store and use herbs effectively over the long term. Although they may sound intimidating, they are probably the easiest preparations to make.

Then there are the close relatives of the tincture: bitters. These tend to focus more on promoting digestion (as an aperitif or digestif) and showcasing a flavour or flavour combo (though not always), and they take a little extra craftsmanship to make…though not much. Tinctures, on the other hand, usually don't taste very good (I'm being honest here). Some herbs, when simply extracted, are very tasty (such as agrimony, hops or sumac). Tinctures also steep (or 'macerate') much longer than bitters, which are made overnight.

**Another difference between tinctures and bitters: with the former, you'll want the highest proof possible for optimal extraction of herbal compounds.** In these instances, a good grade Everclear or vodka tends to be favourable (it should be a clear alcohol). With bitters, however, you can use other types of liquor, even flavoured or non-clear types such as gin, rum, whiskey, tequila or bourbon.

For the best tincture-making ratios, and creating high-quality extractions and products, I can't recommend Richo Cech's *Making Plant Medicine* enough to get those skills fine-tuned. The book discusses all the possible types of compounds in herbs, the best ways to extract them, and the best ratio of alcohol to water.

For quick creations that will still have good benefits for home use and preserve your herbs for upwards of 10 years, however, this simple recipe will be more than adequate.

For any of these tinctures, take as little as 15-30 drops as needed or per day, or 1-2 dropperfuls per day or per setting for healing benefits. **Make sure to educate yourself about the potential side effects, warnings, or interactions noted under each herbal monograph.**

For digestive bitters, take a few drops (on tongue or in drinkable glass of water) before or after meals to boost digestion.

## BASIC TINCTURE OR EXTRACT

**STEP 1** – Make sure your herb is well processed, meaning it is dried all the way down, leaves removed from stems, or better yet ground down or minced into a powder or chopped as finely as possible. This will assist in extracting all the right compounds into your tincture.

Tough roots, seeds or nuts may require additional processing with a grinder or food processor. You can use herbs of all kinds in their fresh form for tinctures.

**STEP 2** – Place the herb in a clean Mason/Kilner jar or other container that is food safe and airtight. Pour your high-proof alcohol over the herbal matter until it's substantially submerged, but not so much that there is significantly more alcohol than herbal matter. (I find that roughly 1 part herbal matter to 1.5–2 parts alcohol works well.)

If you are tincturing dry herbal matter, add a splash of water. Many herbs have a diversity of compounds, some extracted in alcohol and some in water (either alcohol or water soluble) so a little extra water to make up for the loss of an herb's natural water weight helps. Alcohol does contain some water to help with cold water extraction of these compounds, too.

**STEP 3** – Store the jar in a cool, dark place for one month. Whenever you think of it, give it a good shake. This can help loosen compounds for infusion and extraction.

**STEP 4** – After a month, put the tincture through a fine strainer or cheesecloth into a separate clean container. Store it in a dark place, preferably in dark amber glass containers (blue or green work well too). I recommend using dropper bottles for tinctures and keeping them there when the tincture is complete. This makes them easy to use and readily available, taking drops or droppers here and there at a time.

## BITTERS RECIPES

Most bitters are made with a focus on digestion. They can incorporate digestion-forward herbs like lemon balm, angelica, hops and culinary classics like mint, fennel or ginger.

**STEP 1** – Make sure your herb is well processed, meaning it is dried all the way down, leaves removed from stems, or better yet ground down or minced into a powder or chopped as finely as possible. This will assist in extracting all the right compounds into your bitters.

Tough roots, seeds or nuts may require additional processing with a grinder or food processor. You can use herbs of all kinds in their fresh form for tinctures and bitters. If you're making bitters with multiple herbs, make sure you choose herbs that will taste good together and that, to an extent, share similar health properties too. Many people add strongly flavoured foods, spices and seasonings to bitters to enhance their flavour profile: orange zest, lemon juice, fruits, star anise or even smoked salts.

**STEP 2** – Place all the ingredients in a clean Mason/Kilner jar or other container that is food safe and airtight. Pour alcohol over the ingredients until they are substantially submerged.

**STEP 3** – Store the jar in a cool, dark place overnight. Give it a good shake a few times when you remember it.

**STEP 4** – The next day, put the bitters concoction through a fine strainer or cheese-cloth into a separate clean container. Store your bitters in a dark place, preferably in dark amber glass containers (blue or green work well too).

Just like with tinctures, I recommend using dropper bottles with bitters and keeping them there when the tincture is complete. This makes them easy to use when you need them, taking drops or droppers here and there at a time, such as an aperitif or digestif before and after meals.

# Harvesting Herbs

Herb and supplement companies exist to meet your herbal healing needs: loose leaf teas, teabags, sifted spices, tinctures, extracts, syrups… the list goes on. Still, pretty much every acolyte reaches a point where they wish to explore sourcing their own, often in addition to or for the purpose of making their own products. Harvesting herbs for personal use or self-care, also called 'wildcrafting', can be one of the greatest delights for the budding or expert herbalist. It can help you feel more in control of your health, wellness, vitality and nutrition.

You can wildcraft your own herbal remedies and personal medicines, or you can take things a step further and grow your own cultivars. (You may also wish to become the steward of a local weed patch or other natural area.) While harvesting herbs may seem like a straightforward and intuitive process, there are more than a few things that first-time herb harvesters should know before they get started. In this section, you will find basic guidance and how-to's for the most common category of herbal parts.

# Guidance on harvesting herbs in urban areas

Live in the city and wonder if harvesting herbs is possible for you? The answer is yes, it's absolutely possible – but you must be mindful of waste sites, contamination and pollution. Obviously, many urbanites grow gardens or plots without a hitch, picking and harvesting herbal remedies that are clean, pure and without contamination from chemicals in the soil or air. These, in the end, are perfectly safe for consumption. However, it does require one to be mindful of the plot and placement of one's garden area. Strategy in where you plant is very important.

It's best to grow and nurture your herbs away from roads, especially well-travelled ones where smog and pollution could settle on your plants (and thus into your body when you consume them). When growing your own herbs, be mindful of where your home (if planting in the ground) is located. Is it in a recent waste site? Did there used to be a home there? Is it downhill from a road or train track? You're safer not growing into the ground directly, and better off sourcing your own potting soil and cultivating herbs in raised beds far above the ground and away from contamination. If you are not sure about the safety of the site, you can test the soil for heavy metals, radioactive materials, and contaminants before you begin.

If you're not growing your own herbs, you might be surprised at the number of wild plant varieties in your city or neighbourhood that have medicinal qualities – such as stinging nettle, sumac and pine. Regardless, the above considerations apply to wild herbs you find in the city too. Avoid harvesting from plants near roads or downhill from suspicious chemical- or pollution-laden areas. If harvesting from a public park, it's wise to get in touch with the authorities to find out if they spray certain areas (and to check whether it is acceptable to harvest herbs from the park to begin with). Runoff from high spray areas – like lawns, golf courses etc. – are something to consider too.

Be especially wary of thick clumps of annual herbs growing near waste sites in cities. While these may look absolutely tantalizing because of the sheer volume growing in one place (this is especially common with herbs like the European species of stinging nettle), these 'clumps' are often evidence of a high accumulation of harmful chemicals or heavy metals. You will want to avoid harvesting from these, as it's likely these herbs are acting as 'bio-accumulators' sucking up chemicals from the earth, which you will then consume.

# Guidance on harvesting herbs in rural areas

If you live near a pristine natural area, such as a national or state park (or wildlife refuge), it may feel like the world is your oyster when it comes to herb harvesting. And that may be true. You're more likely to find a wide variety of healing herbs in the wild, as well as mushroom healers like lion's mane in untouched wilderness. But that's not to say there won't be barriers to wildcrafting in rural areas.

The same rules apply to the country, especially if you live near agricultural areas. Make sure to consider not only chemical runoff or pollution from roads or waste sites into wild areas you may be harvesting from, but also look out for the runoff from farm fields and ditches. These can pose health hazards through the very plants you wish to pick for the purpose of healing.

If you have a lot of natural wilderness at your disposal – such as mountains, desert, forest, prairie or wetlands – it's also wise to make sure that the harvesting of any herb in these areas is *allowable*. Even without signs posted, walking off-trail in a public park or wildlife refuge could damage plant species or other wildlife. If it's not your own property but is a public area, always enquire with the government or local body managing the area if foot traffic is admissible. Do not trespass onto private property in search of herbal remedies without obtaining the owner's express permission.

# Guidance on harvesting herbs respectfully, sustainably and ethically

Especially when harvesting herbs from the wild, be mindful of how much you are harvesting; this can apply when harvesting herbs in your own garden, too. Clearly, pulling out or depleting your plot will mean fewer herbs and a less vibrant patch in the future. The same goes for wild herbs. Ask yourself how much of the herb you really need. Will others (including animals and other wildlife) be depending on or using the herbs growing here too?

While it can be tempting to harvest all the herbs you find (especially when finding a more elusive herb, and especially when you are harvesting its roots), good ethics among herbalists insist that you take only what you need – and be mindful of the wild population to ensure that it can continue to be just that: a wild, self-sustaining population that will thrive and produce herbal remedies for years to come. If overharvested or stressed, you put the source of your very herbal health and wellness at risk – not just the wellbeing of the plant population.

The health and welfare of a wild stand of herbs is something to take into consideration if you want to wildcraft your home remedies in the most respectful way. Avoid overharvesting from any population, small or large. Be particularly careful of overharvesting from a single plant: its seeds, flowers, leaves, aerial parts or fruiting parts especially, which plants need to both feed themselves and reproduce. When picking your remedies from a population, try to spread out what you take from the population instead of concentrating on one particular area.

**A good hard-and-fast rule is to only take up to one third of the available harvestable parts or plants (if harvesting roots) from a population – and only take up to one third of the available seeds, flowers, berries or fruit from a single plant at a time, or from that population.** If harvesting the full one third, avoid harvesting from that population or patch for a while to give it time to recover and replenish.

Herbalists are often drawn to working with plants knowing full well they're creating relationships with living things – and living things deserve respect. Harvesting respectfully, in the work and practice of many herbalists, is integral to building a relationship with any plant or remedy.

In the beliefs of some, this relationship can even ensure or enhance the potency of the preparations you make with them. In the spirit of ancient herbalist practices that involve magick or spiritualism too, some may even turn to certain traditions for honouring or thanking plants that they harvest from – leaving gifts, offerings or tokens with the plants as a 'thank you' or respectful trade to be able to experience their medicines. Herbalists of many backgrounds have their own rituals around this, based on ancestry or culture, or they may develop personal rituals.

One of my favourite offerings (when harvesting seeds, fruits or berries) is to take a pinch of the berries, seeds, fruits or even fruiting bodies (in the case of wild mushrooms) of whatever I'm harvesting and spread them to new areas – unless they are more invasively inclined. My trade is to aid them in their reproduction process, helping them strengthen or expand their population, and also to ensure there is more life for them – and more herbal remedies for me and others – for years to come as part of our symbiotic herbalist-herb relationship. If you are seeking an equitable ritual, this one has a spiritual and logical basis.

# Harvesting herbal 'aerial parts' (leaves, stems, whole herb etc.)

Most herbs you'll harvest and work with will be made up of 'aerial parts' – the above-ground portion of the plant, usually leaves and stems of a tender nature (such as agrimony, mugwort, plantain or lemon balm). In some cases, it means leaves only, especially if the herbal twigs and branches are of a tougher nature – such as with pine needles, the 'leaves' of the pine tree, which are harvested while leaving the tougher twigs behind (though that doesn't necessarily mean these tougher parts don't have healing properties too).

If harvesting the entire aerial part of a plant (the whole herb, down to the root), use plant cutters or a strong knife to cut the main stem of the herb right down and close to the ground. Remove the whole herb, and use as directed in your preparation. If only leaves are to be used (as in the case of pine), harvest these individually from the plant by hand without cutting out the entire plant – which would be a challenge with a plant like pine, anyway.

# Harvesting herbal flowers

If the herb in question is a tender annual or perennial, harvesting flowers tends to be a breeze (and this is usually the case for the feature flower remedies in this book, arnica and hops). You can gently remove blossoms from stems with your thumb and forefinger, taking care to leave around two-thirds of the flowers or blossoms so that the herb you are harvesting from can still reproduce with its seeds.

If it is a tougher-stemmed plant, scissors or gardening snips can be helpful for removing flowers – roses from rose bushes are a good example. Hops flowers (the cones or 'strobiles' considered a flowering part of the vine) can have a tougher nature in some cases, and have an easier time being harvested with a sharper tool. Some herbalists favour putting their flowers in a shallow wicker or reed basket, being careful to layer blossoms only one layer deep and using the basket to hold the flowers as they air dry naturally.

# Harvesting herbal seeds

Harvesting seeds is very similar in spirit to harvesting herbal flowers.
In most cases they can be easily removed by hand, and with a simple
plucking of your fingers, seed by seed into a container. Herbs with monographs in this book – like stinging nettle, angelica and milk thistle – have
harvestable seeds. Some herbalists prefer to cut whole flowers or drupes,
and then hang them to dry, just like herbal aerial parts; removing the seeds
may be easier when they are dried. This is often the way milk thistle seeds
are harvested, dried and stored for later use or herbal preparation (see p.
146 for harvesting method). That said, drying the seeds isn't necessary,
unless you would like to store them for the long term in your cabinet or
apothecary. Otherwise, if you have the patience, freshly harvested seeds
have amazing potency compared to dried, including stronger aromatic
compounds, oils and phytochemicals (especially with fragrant remedies,
like angelica). The only downside: the harvesting of fresh seeds takes
longer. In the case of harvesting dry seeds, removing the flower to dry the
seeds can be easier using a sharp knife, scissors, or plant cutter rather than
just your hands.

# Harvesting herbal berries or fruits

You'll find that harvesting herbal berries and fruits has a lot in common with seeds, although it's a much easier process thanks to the larger average size of these plant parts. This book's exemplary berry remedy, sumac, grows in clusters, or 'drupes', that are simple to process and create with, and without having to remove all berries to be effective. With other herbal fruits, however – such as elderberry or hawthorn (not explored in this book) – berries tend to be easier to remove from their stems or drupes, and it is preferred to use them that way. Just as in seeds, tougher drupes to remove (such as sumac) may be easier and more convenient with the help of a sharp tool. In more tender plants, fruits or berries can be easily removed and picked with one's fingers. After harvesting, it is often recommended to use most fruits and berries right away; otherwise, dry them (if possible), though this may sap some berries of their medicinal qualities. Because of their combined sugar and water content, fresh herbal fruit or berry remedies simply don't have much of a shelf life, and are best preserved in syrups, vinegars or tinctures.

# Harvesting herbal roots

Herbal roots rank among the most powerful remedies you can harvest, preserve and use for self-care and healing. In exchange for their incredible benefits and potency, they may involve the most work to extract – or more accurately, to exhume (dig up). One of this book's feature root remedies, comfrey, will almost certainly require a shovel or spade; it has a long taproot that delves deep into the ground. Valerian is a similar root remedy that grows deep – and, as a rule, the larger the root is, the more time and digging it will take to pull up.

Garlic, on the other hand, tends to be a shallow cultivated grower. Still, many growers harvest these bulbs with the aid of a shovel or, at the very least, a hand spade. In some cases, the earth is soft enough to pull these combination pot-herb/vegetables from the ground with little to no effort.Upon removal, you will want to remove by hand any clumped dirt from herbal roots, or rinse or scrub it away before using it fresh in preparations or drying it for storage. With all root remedies, the best time to harvest is in the autumn or early winter, when plants send the most energy to their underground systems. This means that the root is more likely to have plentiful compounds for health, healing and nutritive purposes too. Some herbalists choose very early spring as their second choice time for harvesting herbal roots.

# Harvesting mushroom fruiting bodies

Mushrooms are becoming popular herbal remedies in a lot of circles. As such, it's important to know how to properly harvest these medicinal treasures. This book's resident fungal healer, lion's mane, is only one example among many well-reputed, wellness-boosting mushrooms including cordyceps, reishi, maitake, chaga, shiitake and more that unfortunately could not be fully explored in this book. Though obviously these are not plant remedies, they can be compared to plants in that the fruiting body (the most easily and commonly used medicinal part) is much like the fungi's 'flower'.

With some delicacy and finesse, harvesting tender mushroom fruiting bodies (e.g. lion's mane, maitake, shiitake, portobello, etc.) takes only your thumb and forefinger. Regardless of the species, find where the tender 'stem' of the fruiting body emerges from the tree bark, wood chips, or other medium. Pinch tightly and pull away to remove. With tougher mushroom fruiting bodies (such as reishi, but especially for chaga mushroom), you may need a strong knife or hatchet to harvest in the same way: removing the fruiting body from the tree at its base, but with more sustained effort.

A note on wildcrafting mushrooms: be sure to introduce yourself to wild healing mushroom remedies with the help of a local guide or expert before wildcrafting them on your own. There are far too many poisonous lookalikes, and mushroom harvesting can end badly – even in death – due to naiveté. It is essential that you learn or are guided by failsafe identification first.

# Herbal Monographs

Explore these 16 herbs that I (and other herbalists) have found so much joy working with on a culinary level, a self-healing level, or both. I couldn't possibly fit everything there is to know and every possible healing benefit into this book, so I hope readers are satisfied with these introductions – helped along (hopefully) by sharing my personal experiences with them as briefly and as helpfully as I can.

**A quick, handy guide to using this section as an easy reference:** In each herbal monograph, you will find recommendations of the parts to use and the best preparations to use with each of these plants or mushrooms. Look at the 'Parts Used' section under each herb, and cross-reference with the 'Harvesting Herbs' chapter, depending on which part of the remedy you are harvesting, to find basic instructions. Look at the 'Best Preparations' section under each entry, and cross-reference with the 'Basic Herbal Preparations' chapter to find instructions on how to make a basic remedy (or more than one type of remedy) of said herb or mushroom.

**Keep the possibility of contact or food allergies to any of these herbs in mind when using them internally.** I'd recommend using a small patch or skin test beforehand, to see what happens first. If your skin becomes inflamed, I would avoid using the herb altogether because yes, allergies and severe reactions are possible. If at any point, internal use of an herb is causing nausea, vomiting, confusion, stomach upset or other symptoms of bad food reaction, discontinue its use immediately.

**Included under each profile entry are some interesting and more specialized (to the plant) preparations or recipes contributed by herbalists, chefs and other experts I know and look up to.** Some of my own are included in the mix. While I don't claim strong ownership over any of my herbal recipes, some of these preparations are the herbalist's or specialist's own iterations of preparations that are as old as humanity – while others are branded as their own inventions, or methods they have taken pride in developing. Keep this in mind and with respect as you create.

# Glossary of herbalism terms

The following terms will be shown under each herbal profile, designating a general overview of the purported health benefits of each herb. These terms are often used by herbalists. Reference this section to get acquainted with what each herb can do.

**ADAPTOGEN** – May help the body 'adapt' to stress, inflammation, ageing and disease (somewhat synonymous with immune-boosting or tonic).

**ALTERATIVE** – May help support detoxifying functions of the body through kidneys and liver, 'blood cleanser'.

**ANALGESIC** – May help reduce mild pain. (Also called 'Anodyne'.)

**ANTI-ALLERGIC** – May help support the body when dealing with allergies.

**ANTIBACTERIAL** – May help support the body when dealing with bacterial infection.

**ANTIBIOTIC** – May help support the body when dealing with infection from bacteria, fungi, protozoa or other living microorganisms by making the bodily environment unlivable temporarily.

**ANTI-DIABETIC** – May help the body better regulate blood sugars.

**ANTI-DIARRHOEAL** – May help support symptoms of diarrhoea.

**ANTIFUNGAL** – May help support the body when dealing with fungal infections or overgrowth.

**ANTIHISTAMINE** – May help the body reduce a mild histamine or allergic response (e.g. pet dander, seasonal allergens, pollen etc.)

**ANTI-INFLAMMATORY** – May help soothe or fight inflammation.

**ANTI-MICROBIAL** – May help the body expel or destroy any foreign microbes or pathogens (bacteria, viruses etc.)

**ANTI-PARASITIC** – May help support the body in expelling parasites.

**ANTISEPTIC** – When used topically or on surfaces, may help partially or completely destroy pathogens that could be harmful or cause infection (bacteria, viruses etc.)

**ANTI-SPASMODIC** – May help the body reduce muscle contractions and spasms, e.g. cramping.

**ANTI-VIRAL** – May help support the body when dealing with viruses or viral infections.

**ASTRINGENT** – Dries, tightens, 'contracts' and tonifies on contact or after consumption of either tissues or skin (think of the actions of a 'skin toner' versus emollient action). Also denotes anti-diarrhoeal digestive support.

**CARDIOTONIC** – Supports cardiovascular health (blood vessels, blood pressure, arterial walls etc.)

**CARMINATIVE** – May relieve gas and flatulence.

**DECONGESTANT** – May help the body relieve upper respiratory congestion.

**DEMULCENT** – Similar to emollient but specifically effective against inflammation (may also denote laxative action).

**DIAPHORETIC** – May help the body break a fever, typically administered in the form of a hot tea, infusion or decoction.

**DISCUTIENT** – May help disperse 'stuck' tissue or matter in the body; usually applies to blood clots or bruising.

**DIGESTIVE BITTER** – May promote digestion by stimulating release of peptides, bile flow, or reintroducing natural digestive enzymes.

**DIURETIC** – May help promote urination, which may support detoxification, liver health, kidney health, purify the body's lymphatic system and reduce gall or kidney stones.

**EMMENAGOGUE** – May help the body trigger the end of the menstruation cycle (bring on period – a side effect of phytoestrogen).

**EMOLLIENT** – For topical herbs, helps soften and moisten skin (versus astringent action). May also denote some laxative action.

**EXPECTORANT** – May help the upper respiratory tract (lungs, sinuses, mouth, throat etc.) produce and/or move phlegm to aid in fighting an infection or dealing with upper respiratory symptoms.

**FEBRIFUGE** – May help cool or reduce a fever.

**GALACTAGOGUE** – May help stimulate lactation in women while pregnant (side effect of phytoestrogen).

**HEPATOPROTECTIVE** – May help protect the liver from acute damage, such as from poisonous plants or fungi, chemicals, medications, alcohol, toxins etc.

**HYPOTENSIVE** – May help support the body in naturally lowering blood pressure.

**IMMUNOMODULATOR** – May help the immune system balance itself, which can be helpful for autoimmune issues.

**IMMUNOSTIMULANT** – May acutely trigger an aggressive immune response from the immune system to fight an infection or other threat.

**MUCILAGINOUS** – Produces or secretes plant mucilage that has soothing emollient, expectorant, demulcent or laxative action.

**NERVINE** – Helps support the nervous system, especially with anxiety or depression (nerve tonic; may have sedative properties).

**NEUROPROTECTIVE** – May help support the brain, nervous system and neurons against ageing, inflammation, neurological diseases or other symptoms and issues.

**NOOTROPIC** – May help enhance mental energy, cognitive function, learning, memory and other brain functions.

**PHYTOESTROGEN** – Mimics human estrogen in the body and can thus activate estrogen receptors, which when purposeful may have benefits for health (for both men and women, depending).

**RUBEFACIENT** – May increase redness or inflammation in the skin, or bring blood flow to a specific area.

**SEDATIVE** – May have a soothing effect on the nervous system, helping relieve stress, anxiety or sleep issues (also called narcotic, soporific, hypnotic).

**STYPTIC** – When used topically, may help reduce or stop blood flow in wounds until one can find first aid or professional wound care.

**TISSUE REGENERATOR** – May support or enhance the body's ability to grow new tissue, bone, tendon and muscle in a certain rate or timeframe.

**TONIC** – Full of vitamins, minerals, antioxidants and/or phytochemicals that, when consumed daily, boost overall health in some way (or many ways), or may boost immune system.

**TUSSIVE** – May help relieve cough symptoms.

# Agrimony
## (Agrimonia eupatoria, other species)

ENERGETICS
**Cool and Dry**

FLAVOUR
**Sour, Slightly Sweet**

PARTS USED
**Aerial (flowers, leaves, tender stems)**

BEST PREPARATIONS
**Tincture, Extract or Bitters. Also Tea or Infusion, Poultice,
Vinegar or Shrub; Tincture, Extract or Bitters**

PROPERTIES
**Anti-allergic, Astringent, Febrifuge, Hepatoprotective, Styptic**

Agrimony is one of those herbs for which I have personal testimony to its marvels, which quickly vaulted it to the top of my favourites list throughout both my training and personal use. It is not an herb you will find in the 'classic' books, or talked about too much in introductory herbal reference guides. For more about this sidelined European native that has harmoniously naturalized to North America, I highly recommend herbalist Matthew Wood's book *The Book of Herbal Wisdom* (and about its close and similar relative, cinquefoil, as well); he has the same to say about agrimony's lack of fame – which is truly remarkable, considering its wonders.

I like to call certain herbs 'edge walkers' if they prefer to grow where forests start to mingle with grasslands, prairie or other more open environments. That is precisely where I first found agrimony myself (there are other species besides *Agrimonia eupatoria* that have similar uses and growing habits in the wild too). My first encounter with agrimony was delight in recognizing it in the wilds and tincturing it (the best way to use it) immediately. My expectations around the herb, and using it often or noticing powerful effects, were quite low. I was simply interested in collecting it at first – until it completely shattered my expectations.

The tinctured aerial parts of agrimony (less so a hot tea or infusion) have an aroma much like peach, apricot or strawberry: faintly fruity and little sour. I fell in love with its flavour first, which shines brightest in tincture form. A few drops add pleasant subtle flavours to fruity or citrusy drinks. On a whim, knowing it supports the liver, I happened to add a few drops to some juice while my fiancé at the time was dealing with an allergic reaction and itchiness. Its soothing effects were so immediate, I couldn't believe it, and neither could he. (Disclaimer: this benefit from agrimony is just a personal experience. It is highly possible that, based on your constitution, or differences from preparation to preparation, you will have a different experience.)

For the already seasoned herbalist or herbal practitioner, agrimony has a lot of similarity to peach leaf for the liver, inflammation and allergies – peach being another herbal remedy that I love, but that did not make it into this book. Of note, agrimony can also be a topical remedy for healing wounds and stopping bleeding until one can find first aid or professional wound care. It has strong lore and background in homeopathic healing, where it was used as a heart and blood tonic, gallbladder support, liver support and for digestive or diabetic issues that other herbalists have had their own experiences with.

**Warnings before use:** no major considerations, though avoid consuming large quantities of the plant in one sitting (this could only be done intentionally, and would probably be an unpleasant process; it is not likely to happen by accident). Because it's high in the astringent plant compound known as tannins, it could cause some gastric upset if this is done.

# EAR RING #2
## TRILBY SEDLACEK, GREEN ANGELS HERBS & HEALING ARTS
## – CEDAR RAPIDS, IOWA

Agrimony could be considered a very 'clinical' herb, so I thought this recipe 'formula' (using agrimony tincture) provided by a clinical herbalist would be a perfect pairing. Agrimony is often used as a gentle support for major issues relating to the liver or gallbladder – but also, in homeopathic tradition, for tinnitus (also called ringing in the ears). Some herbalists connect tinnitus to the cardiovascular system and blood flow, for which agrimony is considered to be a homeopathic remedy.

For beginning herbalists with ambitions to consult others for health and healing, clinical herbalist Sedlacek – registered with the American Herbalists Guild – provides this tincture formula for support with ear ringing symptoms of tinnitus. It's a fantastic example of an advanced formulation many clinical herbalists get into for creating personalized remedies for people, and which can help give beginner herbalists a taste of formulating. (Warning: Look up side effects and interactions, or speak with your doctor about these, agrimony and any other herbs you plan to take regularly.)

## Ingredients:

✧ Agrimony tincture (30ml)
✧ Bee balm tincture (100ml)
✧ Fresh lobelia vinegar (30ml)
✧ Ginkgo biloba tincture (60ml)
✧ Vinca minor tincture (60ml)
✧ Gotu kola tincture (60ml)

Directions: Take 15-20 drops in a small amount of water 2-4 times per day. If tinnitus improves, discontinue.

Says Sedlacek: 'Frequently, I add Flower essences to my formulas. This one I've added Agrimony, Pear flower or Rescue Remedy, approx. 4 drops for 60ml bottle.'

# Aloe Vera
## (Aloe vera barbadensis)

ENERGETICS
**Cool and Damp**

FLAVOUR
**Subtly Bitter**

PARTS USED
**Latex-Free Inner Leaf Juice (internal or topical), Inner Leaf Gel or Latex (topical only)**

BEST PREPARATIONS
**Infused Oil (gel), Basic Salve (gel); Cold Tea or Cold Infusion
(latex-free juice only if internally taken) for Compress or Wash**

PROPERTIES
**Anti-diabetic (internal), Anti-inflammatory, Demulcent, Emollient, Mucilaginous**

Aloe vera is ubiquitous. And yet we take it for granted so much – I definitely have, even during my herbalism studies. Look at shampoo or other haircare or skincare product labels, and you're more likely than not to find aloe right there, listed next to other ingredients like shea butter, jojoba oil and others. Its inner mucilaginous gel is amazing at moisturizing and softening both hair and skin, and can help soothe the pain and inflammation of sunburn or first-degree burns (but is not ideal for deeper burns or wounds). While products can be made from it (see the Herbal Preparations sections indicated above), many will say that it's most beneficial when the plain inner gel is used right away.

I was also delighted to discover that when aloe's inner gel is strained into a juice – carefully processed to remove any leaf membranes and gel, which can be extremely laxative internally – it can be combined with water or other fruit juices as a digestive aid and to help regulate blood sugars after or between meals. As functional nutrition, aloe juice (properly sourced or made) can be a supportive remedy for those with blood-sugar issues or diabetes worries. It can also help with constipation since it has laxative and demulcent properties too.

Aloe plants are easy to take care of as a potted houseplant, and difficult to kill once they get to a good size. Tropical desert succulents native to the Middle East and Africa, they enjoy a lot of sun but do very well next to a window in most homes, and require little watering. If you live in a tropical, coastal or desert climate, you could get away with growing aloe in your garden – but watch out, it can be invasive. Any time you have itchy skin, a superficial burn, dermatitis, dry skin or any other mild issue with dry or inflamed skin, follow the lead of other herbalists: harvest a leaf from your aloe plant, cut it open, and place the gel on the affected area.

***Warnings before use:*** There is little to worry about when using aloe topically. If you experience a reaction, of course, discontinue its use. If you are purchasing an aloe juice or aloe inner leaf gel product (or processing your own gel or juice) for internal use, however, take care that the product is latex free, or that you strain any fibre, latex or leaf matter out of your creation.

The laxative action of the gel or high latex can be very uncomfortable. It can also pose dangers to children and pregnant or nursing mothers, so be careful when buying, processing and using. Read labels for indicators of 'anthraquinone free', 'latex free', 'inner fillet only' or 'free of aloin' (aloin is the name of aloe's trademark anthraquinone compound).

## ALOE SUNBURN OR WINDBURN REMEDY
## TINA SAMS, AUTHOR AND OWNER OF *ESSENTIAL HERBAL* MAGAZINE

Says Sams, herbalist and published author of many fantastic herbal healing books on this simple aloe vera recipe: 'I used this on my little one. But at the time, I used lavender essential oil. The hydrosol [or distillate] is much better.'

Hydrosols and distillates are amazing herbal creations that I did not include in this book, as I have very little experience or mastery with them. I would highly recommend getting acquainted with Sams' books and even the back catalogue of *The Essential Herbal* Magazine to learn more about hydrosols. If you plan not to make or use a hydrosol, or do not have lavender essential oil available, using just the aloe is perfectly acceptable.

### Ingredients:
- ¼ cup aloe gel with as few additives as possible
- ¼ cup lavender hydrosol (or essential oil)

**STEP 1** – Place the gel and hydrosol in a measuring cup and blend until it is emulsified and liquid.

**STEP 2** – Pour into a 100ml spray bottle and apply liberally. This removes the heat and pain almost on contact.

Adds Sams: 'If you happen to have spent the day snorkelling on a tropical island, chances are there will be giant aloe plants around. Cut a leaf and apply the gel directly to the sunburned areas. With luck, this will save your vacation.'

# Angelica (Angelica archangelica/ Angelica sinensis)

ENERGETICS
**Warm and Dry**

FLAVOUR
**Sweet, Aromatic**

PARTS USED
**Seeds, Stems, Root (dried only)**

BEST PREPARATIONS
**Tea or Infusion (seeds or stems); Syrup, Vinegar, Shrub, Tincture, Extract, Bitters**

PROPERTIES
**Anti-spasmodic, Carminative, Digestive bitter, Diuretic, Expectorant , Febrifuge, Phytoestrogen, Tussive**

Angelica is a tall, spindly, towering flower that has attracted me as a herbalist for many reasons. Admittedly, I have had far fewer encounters with its fragrance and beauty than I would like. It has a wealth of both use and folklore backing it, linked to a shamanic ancestral past of Europe that has been mostly lost through colonization of the continent's distant ancestors (through *Angelica archangelica*). At the same time, in *Angelica sinensis* (also called dong quai), it has long had a hold in eastern Asian healing practices as well, such as in Ayurveda or Traditional Chinese Medicine, and there it has a stronger role as a support herb for women's wellness.

On that note, I have taken up the habit of steering those interested in the Native American and imperilled herb black cohosh for feminine health (owing to its high phytoestrogen content) toward angelica or dong quai instead. Both herbs are also phytoestrogen-rich, have comparable benefits for women's health, and do not suffer the same cultural or environmental issues.

Angelica is a spiritual, digestive and female health remedy. From one herbalist, I learned that the herb was said to be a Celtic favourite for aiding the process of grieving. It also has similar flavourful compounds to herbs I've loved to work with prolifically, such as sweet Cicely, as well as culinary herbs like fennel, anise or lovage, each having at least one thing in common: a sweet liquorice cordial-like flavour. This delightful taste in and of itself is the sign of carminative, anti-spasmodic and digestion-supporting compounds in a herb.

*Warnings before use:* If using angelica root (not recommended for beginners), make sure it is thoroughly dried before use, as fresh angelica root – while powerful – can be toxic. Angelica or dong quai's high phytoestrogen levels mean that it interferes with women's hormones. It's probably wise for women to avoid taking it if they are pregnant, trying to get pregnant, or are known to clinically or sub-clinically have excess estrogen. Angelica belongs to the carrot plant family, and quite a few of these plants may also cause photosensitivity or 'photo-dermatitis' – if you eat or touch the plant quite a bit; spending time in the sun may cause rash, welts or advanced sunburn. On that note, angelica is also closely related to some very dangerous wild plants. Stick to buying or cultivating your own and avoid wildcrafting it unless you have the guidance of an expert plant identifier with you.

## ANGELICA CORDIAL
## GINNY DENTON, LINDEN TREE HERBALS – ANN ARBOR, MICHIGAN

The seeds or stems of angelica on their own make for an excellent aperitif for stimulating the appetite or helping with digestion after meals as a digestif. This exquisite recipe from herbalist Denton takes the classic digestive tonic or bitters to a whole new level.

### Ingredients:

- ✧ Angelica leaves and stems, fresh
- ✧ Orange slices with peel, fresh
- ✧ Lemon balm, fresh
- ✧ Honey (or sugar) to taste
- ✧ Cinnamon
- ✧ Cardamom
- ✧ Allspice
- ✧ 1-pint Mason/Kilner jar with lid
- ✧ Vodka or brandy

**STEP 1** – Fill the jar ⅔ full with fresh chopped angelica leaves and stems.

**STEP 2** – Add 3-4 fresh orange slices, peel included.

**STEP 3** – Add a handful of fresh lemon balm, chopped medium-fine.

**STEP 4** – Fill the jar to the top with good vodka or brandy (up to you) and add 2 dried allspice berries, 2 cardamom pods and a small piece of cinnamon (about 1 inch long).

**STEP 5** – Cap the jar, give it a good shake, and infuse for about 4 weeks, shaking the jar every few days. Sweeten with honey to taste.

**STEP 6** – Add a tablespoonful to tonic and ice, for a refreshing digestive.

# Arnica (*Arnica montana*)

ENERGETICS
**Warm**

FLAVOUR
**Topical Use Only**

PARTS USED
**Flowers**

BEST PREPARATIONS
**Infused Oil or Basic Salve (see pp. 41 and 47).
Or Tea or Infusion (as topical wash only), Poultice,
Tincture or Extract (all for topical use on unbroken skin only)**

PROPERTIES
**Analgesic, Discutient, Rubefacient**

I've never had the honour of encountering arnica in its natural alpine habitat, even though I've worked with and created preparations from its dried flowers many a time with much success. But if I had, I would have recognized it immediately: a dainty flower with long, pointed, graceful leaves and copious all-yellow daisy-like blooms. It grows in open areas and poor soils at very high elevations, famously in mountainous areas of Europe like the Alps and Spanish mountain ranges. It can only be used topically on unbroken skin (not on open wounds). When taken internally, it is toxic and can be lethal.

My experiences with arnica have been many, and exuberantly positive. Far back in my early farm days, while helping my partner raise hogs, I was left with the tough choice of needing to 'manhandle' a large pig who thought I looked and smelled quite a bit more like food than the food I was actually giving him. Use of arnica salve, mixed with a little turmeric, helped immediately melt away the pain in my bruised hands and knuckles where the giant pig roughed me up. I can't recommend arnica enough for topical pain relief of muscles and bruises. And, working alongside other pain relievers like CBD or bone-knitters like comfrey, you have quite the powerful trio and possibilities with this cheery-looking plant.

***Warnings before use:*** As emphasized in other parts of this monograph, absolutely avoid applying arnica preparations on open skin. That goes for permeable tissues and mucus membranes, too, such as sinuses, eyes or mouth. Internal use can be dangerous, causing heart or breathing issues, and possibly death. Be very cautious and careful with use at home; it may be advisable to avoid using arnica at all with young children.

## ARNICA 'SNAKE OIL' ALL-PURPOSE SALVE
## CHARLES 'DOC' GARCIA, CALIFORNIA SCHOOL OF TRADITIONAL HISPANIC HERBALISM

Garcia, a third-generation *curandero* and herbalist, shares this recipe while mentioning his grandfather's creation of topical remedies from actual snake oil or snake fat (with rattlesnake fat being the most valuable and medicinal). Snake oil had reputed powerful healing properties when used topically on skin. This recipe is also a nod to the 'snake oil' healers of old, who would sell snake oil remedies (such as salves) that were praised as highly effective, but whose reputations became tarnished by bad-intentioned salesmen and irresponsible healers who profited unethically over their own claims, and ruined the reputation of snake oil for quite some time (perhaps forever).

**No, you do not have to use actual snake oil or snake fat.** Though this specific salve recipe nods to this Native Californian tradition.

## Ingredients:
- ✧ Beeswax
- ✧ Olive oil
- ✧ Arnica flowers
- ✧ Marigold flowers
- ✧ White sage (aerial parts)
- ✧ Lavender flowers
- ✧ Eucalyptus essential oil

See pages 41 and 47 in this book, and follow the infused oil process first – then the salve making process next, all while adhering to the recipe ingredients above. Use the book's recommended ratios of herb to olive oil, and oil to beeswax.

Says Garcia: 'Whether it be snake oil, olive oil… the method is the same…if you use a crockpot (on low) or a slow cooker, it should be ready in four to six hours.' While using a slow cooker or crockpot is not my recommended method in this book, it has worked wonders for Garcia.

When done, 'It is strained with cheesecloth and placed in tins or glass containers. The smell is usually pleasant,' says Garcia.

# Comfrey
# (*Symphytum officinale*)

ENERGETICS
**Cool and Damp**

FLAVOUR
**Topical Use Only**

PARTS USED
**Leaves and Root**

BEST PREPARATIONS
**Poultice (see p. 51). Or Infused Oil, Basic Salve,
Strong Cooled Infusion (used as wash or compress),
Tincture, Extract (topical only)**

PROPERTIES
**Anti-inflammatory, Discutient, Emollient,
Rubefacient, Tissue Regenerator**

I remember the first time I 'met' comfrey, watching and
helping a herbalist dig up the plant's root to help with an
ankle sprain. The flower was…towering. Almost six feet
tall, with bright purplish-blue bell-like flowers. When we
got to actually digging up the root, the taproot was nearly
six feet deep as well. It took quite a bit of effort to extract
from the ground, and we still weren't able to pull all of it
up. The labour for such a remedy is well worth the effort,
though. Few (if any) other herbs rival comfrey's reputation for supporting the body's ability to heal muscle,
bone and tendon after an injury when applied to the skin
near the injury site. According to research, it can speed
up cellular regeneration and healing in a measurable way.

Comfrey is an excellent follow-up remedy to, or a combination remedy with, arnica. Fortunately, it is all right to use on broken skin, though you don't want to consume comfrey internally either (or have it enter the blood stream often, or copiously). The plant is high in pyrrolizidine alkaloids, which in large amounts can be harmful to the liver. The leaves can be poulticed or made into topical salves or oils for healing, though the root is the far superior part to use.

*Warnings before use:* There is little to fear from comfrey, even in using the plant as a healer near broken skin (comparative to arnica). However, internal use is not recommended at all due to pyrrolizidine alkaloids and potential liver damage if used excessively or over long periods of time.

## COMFREY ROOT POULTICE
### DEBBIE LUKAS, SISKIYOU MOUNTAIN HERBS – TAKILMA, OREGON

Some herbalists lean toward comfrey topical oils or salves because they make for convenient or sellable products. But most herbalists agree on the science: comfrey root poultice, or even a fresh compress, works best for healing, although leaf salves do have good efficacy.

Says Lukas: 'Comfrey is tricky because of the water content and mucilage.' Indeed, the plant's healing compound that stimulates cellular regeneration (allantoin) is found in the soothing mucilage, which can be partially destroyed when exposed to any heat, even in oil- or salve-making – and the extra water can sometimes make for salves with unpredictable consistency, no matter how much you tweak the ratio of oil to wax.

With a fresh poultice, you sidestep any loss of comfrey's healing compounds. **See p. 51 for further directions on herbal poultice-making.** Or follow Lukas's simple steps right here. As it so happens, Lukas was the very same herbalist who showed me the digging up of comfrey root for my very first comfrey experience, including my first time scrubbing those intimidatingly long (but very healing) roots at her farm in southwestern Oregon.

**STEP 1** – Dig up comfrey root. Wash off all dirt with an unimportant dish scrubber or toothbrush. Be sure to pat and air-dry roots before processing.

**STEP 2** – Grate the amount of comfrey root you think you will need for the topical area. (Or use other processing methods – see p. 51, poultice section). If you have unused root left over, store it in the fridge or planted in a dirt bucket in a cool location. Avoid grating the entire root and storing, unless you are sure you will use several applications of comfrey poultice within a short period of time (a few days), because the root oxidizes quickly once cut.

**STEP 3** – Place the poultice or plaster on the area that needs speedy healing, especially a sprain, bone break or pulled muscle. Cover with a wrap or bandage if desired.

**As an extra note,** it's best to remove and replace this bandage regularly, at least daily, with a fresh bandage and newly ground poultice applied. In the meantime, place the entirety of your comfrey poultice covered and in the fridge if prepared, or grate more and process, as you need to reapply and replace bandaging regularly until the entire poultice is used up, or until you are satisfied with healing.

# Garlic (Allium sativum)

ENERGETICS
**Warm or Hot**

FLAVOUR
**Spicy, Pungent**

PARTS USED
**Root (bulb and cloves)**

BEST PREPARATIONS
**Consumed Raw or Cooked in Meals; Infused Oil (internal),**
**Vinegar (pickled), Tincture, Extract**

PROPERTIES
**Adaptogen, Alterative, Antibacterial,**
**Antibiotic (raw only), Anti-diabetic, Antifungal, Anti-inflammatory,**
**Anti-microbial, Anti-parasitic, Antiseptic, Anti-viral, Cardiotonic,**
**Hypotensive, Immunostimulant, Rubefacient, Tonic**

If you ever become both a farmer and a herbalist (or just one, or either, really), the day will come – or maybe already has come – where you will be absolutely swimming in garlic. At the same time, you can never have too much garlic around. Garlic is the ultimate culinary herb for both flavour and health benefits. It's not just the pungent, gut-punching flavour that makes it a seminal seasoning the world over. Garlic, both on its own and in dishes, is great for boosting overall health, with a special focus on heart health, immune health and even supporting symptoms of colds, flu and other contagious viruses. The most pungent, hottest varieties are thought to contain the most compounds for stimulating blood flow and immunity, but also boast a near-antibiotic quality when consumed raw (don't worry, there are recipes to help with this). These raw garlic 'doses' may help combat stomach bugs in particular.

For herbalists or natural health lovers who find themselves consuming quite a bit of store-bought echinacea, consider simplifying things during the winter and sticking to garlic instead. It, too, helps peak immune function in a way that guards against cold and flu symptoms, much like the famous purple coneflower. While it's true that echinacea is most likely commercially grown for the herbal teas or other products you'd buy at natural food stores or supermarkets (and in this case is not overharvested), echinacea is nonetheless an imperilled prairie flower in the wild nowadays, and there's a slight risk that you could be consuming plants from an overharvested population. Plus, it's a Native American medicine that, while effective, is overused and over-associated with immune boosting, while also being overly commercialized and colonized when other less problematic immune boosters are out there.

That's not to say that there's anything wrong with echinacea. Support your local herbalists that prepare these medicines responsibly, through ethical harvesting or even ancestral lineage to the plant's ancient healing use. You can also learn how to harvest the plant ethically yourself. Or, from time to time, give the much more plentiful cultivated alternative garlic a fair swing instead – this is far preferred, especially if you have white colonizer ancestry.

**Warnings before use:** No major considerations have been found with garlic, especially if you are only enjoying it for healing occasionally while eating it often. That said, if you are using strong preparations of it for health often, and have cardiovascular issues (and even if you are using it for cardiovascular issues), talk to your doctor or other health professional. Garlic has been known to interact with some clotting medications because its benefits and effects on the heart and blood vessels are so powerful at preventing blood clots, and thus reducing risk of heart attack, stroke and more.

Obviously, exercise caution while processing the raw herb. Its pungency can have a burning, spicy effect that's unpleasant if it gets into the eyes or sometimes even just on the skin. Some people (including myself) have also reported that eating large amounts of raw garlic can cause gastric distress, which can be uncomfortable, but usually goes away on its own.

## GARLIC TEA FOR COLDS
### MAGGY RHEIN, FRACTAL BRANCH BOTANICALS – MARSHALL, ARKANSAS

Maggy Rhein is a small farmer of hemp and creator of healing CBD products in the Ozark Mountains. Alongside her hemp crop rows are many rows of garlic, providing a variety of medicinal remedies for her family and community, some of which are shipped to customers around the country.

Says Rhein of this recipe, 'In 2010, my best friend and I spent two months in Xela, Guatemala, working with a women's weaving cooperative. A tiny vegetarian restaurant was our go-to for a decompression space, and we met the owner, Bonifaz. When one of us came down with a summer cold, he took us to his apartment to prepare this basic but miraculous remedy. I was initially put off by the garlic – 'in my *tea?!*' But a mild variety, and the other ingredients, help set off the savoury flavour and make it an enjoyable experience.'

## Ingredients:

- ◇ 1 knuckle ginger
- ◇ 1 cinnamon stick
- ◇ 1 large clove garlic
- ◇ 1 lemon (for juice)
- ◇ Raw honey to taste

**STEP 1** – In a small saucepan, heat a cup or so of water, an inch of ginger, chopped, and one whole cinnamon stick.

**STEP 2** – Peel one large garlic clove, and dent it with your fingernail several times to bruise and open it (or you could smash it, but this is more personal).

**STEP 3** – Once the water has boiled, remove from heat and add garlic and the juice of one lemon. It is important not to boil the garlic so that it preserves some of the healing properties. Cover and let steep for 10 minutes, then pour off into a cup and add raw honey to taste.

# Hops *(Humulus lupulus)*

ENERGETICS
**Cool**

FLAVOUR
**Bitter, Aromatic**

PARTS USED
**Flowers (Cones or 'Strobiles')**

BEST PREPARATIONS
**Tincture, Extract or Bitters (see p. 62). Or Tea or Infusion**

PROPERTIES
**Anti-spasmodic, Carminative, Digestive Bitter, Emmenagogue,
Galactagogue, Nervine, Phytoestrogen, Sedative**

A swig from the most bitter IPA beer is a good introduction to hops – both their flavour and their effects. With so many different varieties now, the taste can range from piney to citrusy, zesty, tropical or just plain bitter. This bitterness explains hops' virtues as a digestive tonic. It can help jump-start (or prime) digestion for before or after a meal – but its other compounds make it a gentle sedative too, fantastic for helping alleviate stress or anxiety. I myself love hops tincture and bitters as a flavouring or adjunct to fruit juices right before bed, to give me a little extra help before sleep, if sleep seems elusive. It also has a wonderful flavour when properly combined with others.

Hop is also noticeably high in phytoestrogens, making it beneficial and therapeutic for women's health or other reproductive or hormonal imbalances in all people. It is a choice I may steer people toward instead of black cohosh, a Native American plant that is imperilled in the wild yet still harvested (and in some cases cultivated) as one of the standard industry supplements for phytoestrogens. Hops have no issues around them, are not imperilled, and are almost exclusively cultivated and plentiful in use as supplements and food all around the world.

***Warnings before use:*** No major considerations apply to using hops, and they are generally considered safe. Though the phytoestrogen effect is lower and lesser than other herbs, it may be best to avoid using hops while pregnant or breastfeeding, or while trying to conceive – paradoxically, however, they have been used to stimulate breast milk, so the final verdict on this is unclear.

## SIMPLE HOPS BITTERS RECIPE

This can go one of two ways. You can make a 'fresh' bitters recipe, or let your cones (preferably completely dried down, but not necessarily) sit in the alcohol menstruum for much longer to technically become a much more potent tincture. While fresh hops can sound alluring – I'm speaking to any beer-brewing readers – I personally prefer drying them completely and processing them into a powder before pouring over the alcohol. This releases the lupulin (hops' active compound and flavour) and tons of flavour right on the spot, not unlike the effect of grinding coffee beans.

I (and many others, I presume) also create any bitters alternative to tinctures in order to take away bitterness and capture a much 'fresher' incarnation of a plant's compounds and flavours (such as with lemon zest). Hop is plenty bitter to start with, however, and is supposed to be. In my observation, by letting it steep longer in a tincture, it doesn't get any more bitter to taste, but it does feel like it gets more potent with time. Meaning: a tincture could still be considered a 'bitters'.

The length of time you decide to let your hops soak or 'macerate' is up to you. Whether you make it into a true tincture or bitters, you're in for a very 'bitter' bitters either way. (See p. 66 for more specifics on bitters creation.)

**STEP 1** – Place hops (preferably dried and processed or powdered) in a clean Mason/Kilner jar or other container that is food safe and airtight. Pour the alcohol over the ingredients until they are substantially submerged. (While Everclear or vodka are great choices, if you're strictly going for flavour and not potency, gin is an excellent pairing with hops.)

**STEP 2** – Store the jar in a cool, dark place overnight. Give it a good shake a few times, when you remember it. If you like, add other ingredients like grapefruit zest, spruce tips, pine needles or even cedar or juniper berries; all of these pair well with hops.

**STEP 3** – The next day, strain the bitters concoction through a fine strainer or cheesecloth into a separate clean container. Store your bitters in a dark place, preferably in dark amber glass containers (blue or green work well too).

Take a few drops or dropperfuls before or after meals to boost digestion or appetite. Or, take a bit before bed, directly on the tongue or in water or juice, to enhance sleep or soothe anxiety.

# Lemon balm (*Melissa officinalis*)

ENERGETICS
**Cool**

FLAVOUR
**Aromatic**

PARTS USED
**Aerial (leaves, tender stems, flowers)**

BEST PREPARATIONS
**Tea or Infusion; Syrup, Tincture, Extract or Bitters**

PROPERTIES
**Analgesic, Anti-spasmodic, Anti-viral, Carminative,**
**Diaphoretic, Digestive Bitter, Nervine, Sedative, Tussive**

I have always wondered why lemon balm isn't a far more famous culinary herb or seasoning, joining the ranks of relatives or similar plants like mint, lemon verbena, or lavender, which are such popular flavours. Lemon balm's taste is divine, with a very subtle coolness classic to mints (it is in the mint family) but with a hint of lemony citrus flavour as well. Even more amazing is lemon balm's ability to untie the butterflies or knots in one's stomach – including mine, many a time – with just a sip from a piping hot tea of the plant, or a few drops of the tincture or bitters for digestive upset, stress, anxiety or nervousness. It is also known to be helpful for soothing the symptoms of mild depression.

Some herbalists claim that lemon balm has mild cold-fighting and anti-viral properties, which makes it an excellent ingredient for topical balm or salve for cold sores. A hot tea can help bring on a fever with mild viral illness, say some, as well as soothe a sore throat. With or without stomach butterflies, it has awesome digestion-supporting abilities. Or, if you're suffering the heat on some scorching summer day, add some sprigs of it to your favourite iced tea, as a garnish to juice, or incorporate it with citrus or fruit in a cooling popsicle recipe. Delectable.

***Warnings before use:*** There are very few reports of lemon balm being unsafe or having side effects, as it is pretty much categorized with close relatives like peppermint or spearmint, which likewise are safe to use and consume freely. Children and women who are pregnant or breastfeeding can safely consume it. Some herbalists use lemon balm to support hyperthyroidism, which may mean it is best not to use it if you have lower thyroid function.

## LEMON BALM TEA
### ADRIENNE MITCHELL, NU MOON HERBALS

Mitchell had lots to say about lemon balm – a herb I can tell she's passionate about, and which I truly feel one can't help but be passionate about once you get to know it. She mentioned multiple studies showing that it is effective in healing HSV1 (topical herpes simplex, aka cold sores) and other lesions, and from other herbalists, too, I have heard that it is one of the best and simplest known herbs for the ailment.

Here, Mitchell shares one of her favourite teas featuring lemon balm, saying, 'This blend in a tea can help reduce stress and promote restful sleep.'

### Ingredients:

- ✧ 2 tbsp. lemon balm
- ✧ 1 tbsp. chamomile flowers
- ✧ 1 tsp. lavender flowers

Steep this blend in hot water for 5 minutes, then strain. Sit with your tea and inhale the steam, as it contains traces of the essential oils and will aid in relaxation. This is a great time to put intent into your tea, and give it extra direction as to how you want it to aid your body.

## SOOTHING AND CENTRING EVERYDAY TEA
## HILLARY SCHOFIELD, AURIFERUM – IOWA CITY

Lemon balm is a popular one. I couldn't resist including an additional recipe for a basic, enjoyable tea from herbalist friend and professional astrologer Schofield. From the spiritual and magickal angle of herbal healing, Schofield as an astrologer had some cosmical tidbits on lemon balm, and this blend as a whole, to share – in the tradition that it was common in ancient times for certain herbal remedies to have astrological significance too.

'The predominant energetics of this blend are of Venus,' says Schofield. 'Venus shows up here as helping to establish equilibrium, smooth out frayed nerves, and bring ease….Looking specifically at lemon balm, in the Western astrological tradition they have most notably been connected with Jupiter and the Sun, reflecting lemon balm's uplifting and vitality-boosting qualities.'

## Ingredients:

 ✧ 3 cups spearmint
 ✧ 2 cups lemon balm
 ✧ Catnip
 ✧ Chamomile flowers
 ✧ 1 cup red clover
 ✧ Nettles
 ✧ Motherwort
 ✧ Oat straw
 ✧ Rosebuds and/or petals
 ✧ Blackberry leaf
 ✧ Lavender
 ✧ Skullcap
 ✧ Marshmallow leaf
 ✧ ½ cup fennel, coarsely ground fresh or powdered
 ✧ ½ cup hawthorn berries
 ✧ ¼ cup orange peel, finely chopped or powdered

Says Schofield, 'All ingredients for this are dried. Amounts shown make about a 3.8-litre batch. You can of course make smaller amounts by dividing the recipe in half (or more). There is a lot of wiggle room with the ratios, and I encourage you to fine-tune it to your tastes. You can also skip some of the herbs if you do not have them, or add others that seem like a good fit. Make it work for you.'

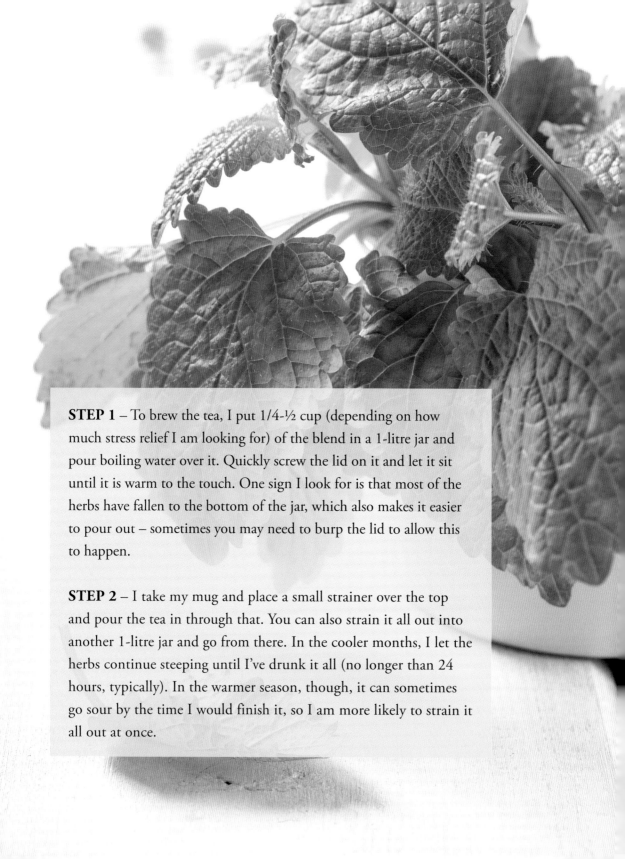

**STEP 1** – To brew the tea, I put 1/4-½ cup (depending on how much stress relief I am looking for) of the blend in a 1-litre jar and pour boiling water over it. Quickly screw the lid on it and let it sit until it is warm to the touch. One sign I look for is that most of the herbs have fallen to the bottom of the jar, which also makes it easier to pour out – sometimes you may need to burp the lid to allow this to happen.

**STEP 2** – I take my mug and place a small strainer over the top and pour the tea in through that. You can also strain it all out into another 1-litre jar and go from there. In the cooler months, I let the herbs continue steeping until I've drunk it all (no longer than 24 hours, typically). In the warmer season, though, it can sometimes go sour by the time I would finish it, so I am more likely to strain it all out at once.

# Lion's Mane
## (Hericium erinaceus)

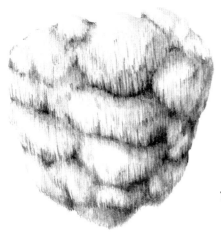

ENERGETICS
**Damp**

FLAVOUR
**Savoury, 'Umami'**

PARTS USED
**Fruiting Body**

BEST PREPARATIONS
**Tea or Infusion; Syrup; Vinegar; Tincture or Extract**

PROPERTIES
**Adaptogen, Anti-inflammatory (chronic inflammation),
Cardiotonic, Hypotensive, Immunomodulator, Nervine,
Neuroprotective, Nootropic, Sedative (mild), Tonic**

Mushrooms were one of many foods I pushed to the edge of my plate as a kid. One day, in my late teens (and during a short fling with veganism), I ate a vegan pizza and was blown away by the flavour. It still managed to be savoury, rich and meaty with absolutely no meat – and it was all because of the mushroom toppings.

I have found lion's mane and other medicinal culinary mushrooms, such as shiitake or maitake, to hold a unique territory in herbalism and plant-based (or fungi-based) healing because of their 'damp' umami nature. A lot of plants simply cannot do what they do. (To read more about 'damp' herbs and constitutions, energetics and the healing lore behind lion's mane, look to traditional Asian healing modalities such as Traditional Chinese Medicine and Ayurveda.)

At a basic level, lion's mane and other mushrooms contain nutrients we need to be healthy, but which are uncommon in plants – while these same nutrients are present aplenty in animal or meat products. For the vegan, vegetarian, or whole-food plant-based eater, they could be an indispensable food. Meanwhile, when it comes to 'food as medicine', mushrooms like lion's mane are unparalleled immune boosters and inflammation-fighters.

I specifically gravitated toward lion's mane when I was in search of a nervine (nervous system support) healer when I was in my mid-twenties. Having a naturally cold and dry constitution, I sought out a nerve healer – any nerve healer – that would be 'damp' and basically more nourishing to my body than other nervines or adaptogens I was looking at at the time. However, most plant nervines are 'dry' and diminishing in nature, even if they were cooling and soothing. How delighted I was to discover lion's mane for my self-care purposes: a mushroom with studies showing it nourishes the nervous system and holistically supports issues surrounding stress, depression, burnout – and may even lower risk of serious neurological issues such as dementia, Parkinson's or Alzheimer's. It also has the added bonus of benefitting the body's fight against inflammation, immune issues, and even supporting heart and blood vessels.

***Warnings before use:*** Lion's mane is a regularly consumed food around the world and doesn't pose any health hazards. Some people may have mushroom allergies, so if you exhibit these, discontinue its use. In rare instances, lion's mane has been shown to worsen other allergies or asthma. People with liver or other digestive issues may have trouble digesting it.

# LION'S MANE ALCOHOL-FREE EXTRACT
## DEBBIE LUKAS, TAKILMA, OREGON

For those with scientific minds, advanced herbalism ambitions, or who want to tap into lion's mane's 'brain power' without the alcohol of tinctures, this recipe (which requires a dehydrator) will be right up your alley.

## Ingredients:

- 500g lion's mane mushrooms (fresh)
- 170g lion's mane powdered fruiting bodies (dried)
- 2.4 litres water (preferably filtered)

**STEP 1** – Simmer the 500g of lion's mane mushrooms in the 2.4 litres of water for 4 to 8 hours.

**STEP 2** – Strain or press out the mushroom material. Return the tea back to a simmer without the mushrooms, and reduce to about 240ml.

**STEP 3** – Add the 240ml of liquid to the powdered dry mushrooms, and spread out on a flat cooking sheet or other container that fits inside your dehydrator (and withstands the temperatures – nothing plastic). Dehydrate at 45°C/110°F for about 24 hours, checking regularly.

**STEP 4** – Use this dried-down mixture of reduced tea and whole dried lion's mane mushrooms as a daily supplement, add as powder to a hot tea, sprinkle atop foods, or even put into capsules.

# Milk Thistle
## (*Silybum marianum*)

ENERGETICS
**Cool**

FLAVOUR
**Bitter**

PARTS USED
**Seeds**

BEST PREPARATIONS
**Seeds eaten raw or as seasoning.
Or Tea or Infusion, Tincture or Extract**

PROPERTIES
**Alterative, Anti-allergic, Anti-diabetic, Antihistamine,
Anti-inflammatory, Carminative, Digestive Bitter,
Hepatoprotective**

In my personal experience I have only had one encounter with milk thistle: making a preparation and recommending it to a friend who was recovering from substance and alcohol issues for its 'liver-clearing' effect. On the whole, however, I'm more in awe of the plant's enormous wealth of research in favour of its 'detoxifying' and liver-protecting uses, which is fully backed up by experiential and traditional herbalist use. So, I just had to include it, especially as one of the plant world's most powerful liver healers – quite possibly the most powerful liver healer in the plant world.

As a herbalist I personally think that just about everyone (not just herbalists) could benefit from a container of milk thistle seeds in their pantry. Because of its amazing effect on the liver (not too unlike agrimony, only more well-studied and possibly more potent) thanks to a compound called silymarin, it can help the body cope with issues of illness to an incredible extent: including excess alcohol consumption, medication overuse, poisoning, animal bites, allergic reactions, a generally unhealthy liver and more. Only a few of these I've been able to witness, while other herbalists have witnessed far more to deem milk thistle a must-have herb for the apothecary. As a bonus, its bitter qualities lend a helping hand to the body when dealing with issues including digestive imbalance, inflammation and allergies.

*Warnings before use:* Milk thistle is widely used around the world, sometimes even in conventional medicine situations. It's been shown to be very safe. That said, some would recommend to people with liver issues or disorders to be cautious with the herb and to talk to your doctor about using it beforehand. If you are dealing with any issues related to poisoning, animal bites, severe allergic reactions, overdoses or accidental ingestion of harmful substances or plants, contact an emergency room immediately and do not solely depend on the use of milk thistle.

## HARVESTING AND DRYING MILK THISTLE SEEDS

In late autumn or summer, when all manner of thistle plants go to
flower and set their seeds, harvest the tops of your milk thistle plants
(whether cultivated or foraged) – ideally with gloves in order to avoid any
uncomfortable pricks. Or, alternatively, pick fresh flowers and hang them
upside down to dry in a cool, dark place until the tops are dry enough for
processing.

Again, preferably wearing gloves (if you're concerned about dried
needles – and I would be), carefully coax seeds out of the dried flower
pods and set these aside in a dry glass container that can be sealed
airtight. Store this container in a dark, dry place. As needed, use
milk thistle seed like a medicinal supplement by chewing about one
teaspoon of seeds as a dose. This can be done daily to support health,
especially liver health. Seeds can also be crushed or ground (possibly
even in some pepper grinders) as a seasoning on daily meals for health
benefits as well.

# Mugwort
# (*Artemisia vulgaris*)

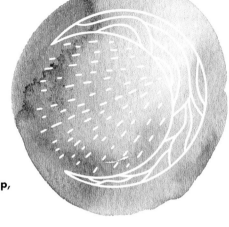

ENERGETICS
**Cool and Dry**

FLAVOUR
**Bitter**

PARTS USED
**Aerial (tender leaves and stems)**

BEST PREPARATIONS
**Tea or Infusion; Infused Oil, Basic Salve, Syrup,
Vinegar, Shrub, Tincture, Extract or Bitters**

PROPERTIES
**Anti-microbial, Digestive Bitter, Dream Enhancer, Febrifuge**

I have always loved having dreams and exploring what they mean. For the more prolific period of my life when I worked doing astrological, psychic, and I Ching readings, dream interpretation and 'dream work' were some of my specialties as well: helping people make sense of what their subconscious or unconscious was telling them (or in some beliefs, what the ancestors or spirit world were telling them). Various herbs can aid people in this type of work, with mugwort being one of the most popular; some could call it the poster child 'dream herb' of Western culture.

Many people report also that mugwort can help stimulate not only more vivid dreaming, but lucid dreams as well. A hot tea, which is quite bitter – helped along with some honey sweetening – is one great way to use it. A vinegar may make its bitterness more palatable. Otherwise tinctures, extract or artfully made bitters could lightly stimulate the dreamtime.

Mugwort has other benefits too. A close relative of the highly bitter plant wormwood – of absinthe fame, and also an artemisia family member, like mugwort – the bitterness of mugwort makes its benefits as a digestive healer a fantastic bonus. I would also encourage people to explore mugwort (along with classic Mediterranean garden sage, *Salvia officinalis*) as a replacement herb for 'smudging' as much as possible instead of turning to the Native American herb white sage or estafiate, for multiple reasons; white sage is also a close mugwort relative (*Artemesia ludoviciana*).

Not only is the wild prairie plant white sage overharvested and heavily commercialized, the use of it for spiritual or cleansing purposes can be seen as problematic. (Especially if purchase of the herb goes to a predominantly white-profiting company or entity.) However, mugwort can be burnt just like white sage, and was used for similar purposes among ancient Europeans to cleanse objects and spaces (called 'saining' in Gaelic). This very same smoke from saining, as it purifies, can encourage a more active dream life when you are in the presence of it and inhaling its fragrant fumes…you might just experience interesting dreams later that night.

***Warnings before use:*** Mugwort is relatively considered safe. Because it stimulates one's dream life and has such a close relation to absinthe psychoactive wormwood, it may be wise to avoid taking it in large doses. Some reported side effects include stimulating uterine contractions, so women may want to avoid internal use during pregnancy, and it is best kept off-limits for children.

## DRIED MUGWORT BUNDLE FOR SMUDGING

Make your very own mugwort smudge sticks for enhancing dream life, purifying a space, or to add ambience to meditation, mindfulness, ceremony, or a simple serene moment. This can be done by harvesting, drying, and bundling the aerial parts of the mugwort plant.

**STEP 1** – Harvest and gather dried mugwort branches. Preference goes to tender-stemmed branches with larger leaves, but if these are scant, use gardening pruners or tough scissors to cut away some of the woodier stems to extract some branches (being careful not to over-harvest from the plant). Ideally, pick branches that are not in flower.

For one full bundle or stick, harvest a bundle of mugwort that fits into the full diameter of the grip of your hand if your fingers were to be completely encircled around the base of the bundle (all four fingers touching the tip of your thumb).

**STEP 2** – Tie the bundle together at the base and hang upside down on a line to dry in a cool, dark place until mostly dry but not completely brittle – still pliable for bundling and wrapping.

**STEP 3** – Take thin, untreated string (free of plastics or chemicals, as this will be burned while smudging) and methodically loop and wrap the string around the bundle from the very base to the tip, so it makes for a nice and tight bundle that won't fall apart easily. You can do this in parallel wrapping patterns, or crisscross patterns.

**STEP 4** – When securely tied and bundled, you're ready to burn your mugwort bundle, starting at the non-stem end. Light with a lighter or matches to emit smoke, smudge, and purify. Make sure to put out any embers completely when not in use.

# Pine *(Pinus strobus)*

ENERGETICS
**Cool and Dry**

FLAVOUR
**Aromatic (resinous)**

PARTS USED
**Leaves (needles) – Sap ('resin') or Pollen**

BEST PREPARATIONS
**Tea or Infusion (see p. 34). Or Infused Oil, Basic Salve,
Syrup, Vinegar, Shrub, Tincture, Extract, Bitters**

PROPERTIES
**Anti-bacterial, Antifungal, Anti-microbial, Antiseptic,
Decongestant, Diuretic, Expectorant, Styptic, Tussive**

While going through my two herbalist training programmes in the early 2010s, I was introduced to pine (and especially white pine) as 'the most powerful antimicrobial healer'. Not too long after this I decided to go walking through my home's nearby evergreen woods in search of some white pine sap early one spring, when the evergreen sap would be running. The key is to look for natural gouges or dropped limbs from the pine's tree trunk that would leave an open wound, some time before most leaves and flowers on deciduous plants would be up and blooming. From these wounds, the white pine's sap will flow – a noticeably bright, milky substance, the tree's healing blood itself, designed to clean and close its own wounds. Without harming, cutting or gouging the tree, you can lightly scrape or collect this sticky sap for healing use right off the bark if you can find it. I've used white pine for many things since then, especially for helping with wound healing, keeping wounds clean and protecting against the risk of infection – even as a mouth wash.

That said, the fresh and tender new pine needles that the tree produces each spring are great for other self-care use too – as are spruce tips, another evergreen tree I've loved to work with and that has similar properties. Either can be used to give things a fabulous gin-like flavour which is supposed to be from juniper, but pine flavour is very similar. When not using the pine resins, fresh tender pine needles from the season's first new growth from the tree can be wonderful to work with too: for creating aromatic cleaners, or even elixirs or bitters that help stimulate the lungs and respiratory tract to deal with coughs, phlegm or congestion.

*Warnings before use:* There's little to no reports on side effects from pine that I could find. Since it is mostly a topical remedy for wound cleaning or cleansing, there is very little risk there. Obviously, any sort of skin reaction means you should stop using it, and it could signify an allergy. Pine is high in tannin compounds that are highly astringent; consuming too much internally in flavoured products or other herbal creations (like a tea) could possibly cause some gastric upset, but most people will probably not drink nearly enough to experience that.

## WHITE PINE CORDIAL
### EMMA BARBER, RHUBARB BOTANICALS IN MT. VERNON, IOWA

While not utilizing white pine's classic wound-healing properties, sometimes the best way to enjoy a herbal remedy is to simply bask in its flavours – just like in this fabulous, tasty cordial recipe. It's a perfect creation to make in the springtime or, really, anytime.

## Ingredients:

- Fresh white pine needles – approx. 3 cups
- 2 tbsp. fresh grated ginger or 1 tbsp. dried ginger
- Peel & pith of 1 orange
- Approx. 600ml of your liquor of choice: gin, vodka, whisky or scotch
- 250ml honey

**STEP 1** – Fill a clean quart-sized glass jar ⅔ full with fresh pine needles.

**STEP 2** – Grate 2 tbsp. fresh ginger and add to the jar, or add 1 tbsp. dried ginger.

**STEP 3** – Cut the peel of one orange into strips and add to the jar, including the white pith.

**STEP 4** – Add other aromatic herbs and spices if you wish. Rosemary, cardamom, cinnamon and/or hawthorn berry would all be excellent choices.

**STEP 5** – Pour the honey over the herbs.

**STEP 6** – Pour your choice of alcohol over the herbs until the jar is full. Stir well with a clean spoon, then put the lid on the jar and shake well.

**STEP 7** – Shake daily or as often as you can remember for one month.

**STEP 8** – Strain the liquid from the herbs and decant into a clean jar or fancy bottle.

**STEP 9** – Sip your White Pine Cordial neat on chilly winter nights for warming respiratory support, or enjoy it with sparkling water over ice for a refreshing spritzer.

# Plantain
# (*Plantago major/Plantago lanceolata*)

ENERGETICS
**Cool and Damp**

FLAVOUR
**Bitter, Salty**

PARTS USED
**Aerial (tender leaves and stems), Seeds**

BEST PREPARATIONS
**Tea or Infusion; Infused Oil, Basic Salve,
(spit) Poultice, Tincture or Extract**

PROPERTIES
**Analgesic, Anti-allergic (topical), Antihistamine (topical),
Anti-inflammatory, Demulcent, Emollient, Expectorant, Mucilaginous , Styptic**

Plantain (no, not the banana relative) has the nickname 'white man's foot' in America for a couple of reasons. Both species listed here came from Europe on the coattails of white colonizers and settlers as they arrived in North America, after which it spread across the land. The other reason: plantain does appear to flourish the more you stomp on it. You'll find that the larger, almond-shaped leaf species *Plantago major* prefers disturbed areas or waste sites, especially the more compact the soil is, such as driveways or walkways. *Plantago lanceolata* has somewhat similar preferences, except it does prefer open fields or pastures a little more if you find a nice patch of plantain that looks relatively non-stomped (for safety and sanitary purposes).

If you have a bug bite or bee sting, pick a leaf from the plant and chew it, then place it on the sting (for more specific directions on this 'spit poultice', see below). In most cases the itch or pain will go away immediately. According to herbalists, this effect is optimized by human saliva, though plantain compresses, oils and salves also have benefits.

I myself had the experience of having plantain nearby after an unfortunate encounter with a yellowjacket nest in the Appalachian mountains. Stung at least 10 times, I found that plantain helped quite a bit with the pain for the next few days. Besides bee stings and itching, however, plantain has an emollient and demulcent action somewhat similar to aloe or comfrey, and can be eaten or taken internally as well as topically. You can also use it in a topical salve to help remove poison ivy oils right after contact, to soothe a sunburn, or to temporarily stop the bleeding of a wound.

As food, I've used raw leaves in smoothies with a focus on cooling detoxification support internally, but I could see a plantain tea helping with raw, unproductive and dry coughs. Of note, plantain is a close relative of *Plantago ovata*, or psyllium seed. The leaves do have a mild laxative effect, and most likely, the seeds even more so. (Though use with caution and at your discretion – I cannot guarantee this is a safe or comfortable experience.)

***Warnings before use:*** Plantain leaf is probably one of the safest and most harmless remedies I've come across. Regardless, be cautious: test it on your skin to see if you have any dermatitis reaction or allergy before chewing it or using it topically. Internally, eating large amounts of plantain could have a laxative effect…this may just be more undesired than unpleasant.

## THE INFAMOUS
## PLANTAIN SPIT POULTICE

Almost every novice herbalist (including myself, when I was just learning) learns the plantain spit poultice, as it is one of the easiest, quickest and most effective tricks to learn for bug bites and bee stings. The relief is immediate, the steps are simple…and the original 'recipe' is attributed to no one. It's just an old-timey herbalist trick.

**STEP 1** – Pick a plantain leaf, and rinse it with cool water first if you like.

**STEP 2** – Chew the leaf; this is essential, as salivary enzymes are key to 'awakening' the antihistamine effects.

**STEP 3** – Spit or place the chewed poultice on the bug bite or sting. You should feel relief from pain or itching in seconds. Rinse away the plant matter once symptoms are gone.

# Stinging Nettle
## (Urtica dioica/Laportea canadensis)

ENERGETICS
**Drying, Slightly Warming**

FLAVOUR
**Bitter, Salty**

PARTS USED
**Aerial (tender leaves and stems), Seeds**

BEST PREPARATIONS
**Tea or Infusion; Syrup, Vinegar, Tincture or Extract**

PROPERTIES
**Adaptogen, Anti-allergic, Antihistamine,
Anti-inflammatory, Decongestant, Diuretic, Tonic**

Anyone who is new to the woods (especially those who didn't grow up near woodlands) has been fearful of stinging nettle and its itching, burning pain upon contact. That includes me, a suburban-raised kid who, though I loved to play in nature, grew up in the southwestern United States and didn't encounter it much until I was an adult. I heard horror stories about stands of it in deeper woods up in the mountains, but never encountered them. Once I became a Midwesterner (where nettle can absolutely fill a forest understory) and travelled around the country more, my encounter came. How ironic that a herb that causes burning pain and dermatitis can be a fantastic plant-based inflammation-fighting food. Apparently, the histamine in its needles may be responsible for this.

Eating it regularly may not only help support inflammation from things like arthritis pain, but also sinus inflammation and congestion. Stinging nettle is also incredibly high in vitamins and minerals for combating fatigue, and that goes for wood nettle (*Laportea canadensis*), the native species to the United States, as well. I myself have experienced a sort of stimulating and clearing energy afterward when consuming it regularly, which I can only credit to its amazing nutrients. This is why stinging nettle has long been recommended for or administered to people who are in need of more energy and less inflammation in their lives – especially those dealing with spring or seasonal allergies. After some time eating and enjoying stinging nettle as a food or medicine, when I've happened to get 'nicked' by some out in the wild, somehow its sting doesn't smart as much for me…and maybe that's due to my appreciation of it.

***Warnings before use:*** Mind the sting while harvesting. Sensitivity to it varies among different people, so use sleeves and gloves while harvesting if you don't want to get stung. Nettle is considered very 'drying' because it is a diuretic, so avoid overusing or overeating it – this can be a little hard on the kidneys and have an opposite nutritive effect in loss of minerals through more frequent urination. There are some concerns that nettles can stimulate uterine contractions, so pregnant women may be wise to avoid it.

## BLACK STRAP NETTLE SYRUP

This is my go-to preparation and method for taking nettles daily for their energetic and nutritive benefits, rather than drinking the bitter infusion daily. The addition of molasses, also high in vitamins and minerals, makes it an even more powerful and pleasant tasting tonic 'supplement'.

## Ingredients:

- ✧ Dried (or fresh) stinging nettles (at least 1 cup)
- ✧ 550-850ml honey (preferably organic; raw is OK)
- ✧ 420-570ml black strap molasses
- ✧ Water

**STEP 1** – Fill a small to medium pot with water. Bring to a gentle simmer, then add the nettles to create the initial infusion. Cover. Let it simmer for a while, until the water is a very dark green. You can leave it to simmer, or just leave it on low heat. The sludgier-looking, the better (more vitamins/minerals). You may add more water if too much evaporates, and infuse as long as you like. It may take a while.

**STEP 2** – Strain out the herb from the infusion and put the liquid in a new, clean pot. Add the honey and bring it up to a simmer again.

**STEP 3** – At this point, you are 'simmering down' your syrup to the consistency you like. This may also take a while. Stir it a bit from time to time. Some syrups can be runnier, with more water content, others can be a bit thicker; it just depends upon the length of simmering. A couple of notes: syrups are runnier at a higher temperature, so it will be a bit thicker when it has cooled. Also, the black strap molasses may increase thickness.

**STEP 4** – Once the syrup has reached the desired consistency, add the molasses to the mixture and stir while it is still hot. Let cool.

**STEP 5** – Add the cooled Black Nettle Syrup to a container, preferably glass and amber-tinted. Make sure to store syrup in fridge when not in use.

# Sumac
## (*Rhus typhina,*
## other *Rhus* species)

ENERGETICS
**Cool and Dry**

FLAVOUR
**Sour, Bitter**

PARTS USED
**Berries**

BEST PREPARATIONS
**Tea or Infusion (cold infusion best for flavour); Syrup, Vinegar, Shrub, Tincture, Extract or Bitters**

PROPERTIES
**Anti-diarrhoeal, Anti-microbial, Antiseptic, Astringent, Diaphoretic, Digestive Bitter, Diuretic, Tonic**

As a kid in the Southwest, I would play in a small stand of sumac bushes thinking they were a jungle or tropical forest, mostly because of their exotic appearance. As an adult studying herbalism much later in the Midwest, I would look upon those graceful shrubs, with their blazing sunset foliage in autumn and bright red berries, and wonder: does this favourite childhood plant of mine, native to North America, have any healing benefits? I was delighted when I found out the answer was yes, not only as a vitamin C-rich infection fighter and microbe killer for oral issues, but also for treating common colds and flu.

If you've explored eastern Mediterranean cooking, you've no doubt heard of powdered sumac berry in za'atar, a Lebanese cooking spice. It can be described as earthy, sour, a little bit fruity and very cooling. As for the native species from North America, sumac berries (especially staghorn sumac, the most flavourful variety native to the United States) are used to make delicious sumac-ade, a beverage of Native American origin. I quickly fell in love with sumac because of its beauty, the childhood connections, and its wonderful, sour flavour – and also because of how good it is for health and healing. It is strongly astringent and anti-microbial (especially the less flavourful but more bitter species of smooth sumac, *Rhus glabra*); and with the plant's help, I was able to speed up my healing after wisdom-tooth surgery, and fight off strep throat.

Even more amazingly, I recommended the plant to a friend, who reported that it helped him sidestep root canal surgery. (Of course, be sure to consult with a dentist about tooth surgery, and don't rely on plants – my friend was a lucky example.) Rich in tannins in the berry drupes' stems and bark, sumac may also support digestive regularity and help fight stomach bugs or pathogens, thanks to its anti-diarrhoeal and anti-microbial properties.

***Warnings before use:*** Few concerns surround sumac, and it can be consumed safely by just about anyone in fairly plentiful culinary or healing amounts. It is a tannin-rich plant, so eating or drinking excessive amounts of the berry may cause some gastric upset. If harvesting in the wild, know the difference between culinary or medicinal sumacs and poison sumac. The poisonous relative has bright white berries and grows in swamplands; make sure you know how to tell them apart, as poison sumac can cause painful rashes.

## SUMAC-ADE
### NICO ALBERT, BURNING CEDAR INDIGENOUS FOODS

Nico Albert of the Cherokee Nation shares this recipe, which allows users access to the easiest, most flavourful and arguably one of the most medicinal (and enjoyable) sumac preparations out there – for which we have indigenous knowledge to thank. Albert's work with Burning Cedar Indigenous Foods aims to restore these same healing and foodways that have been lost through colonization and co-opting: the very foundation to healing I speak of in this book's introductory sections, specifically in 'How Do Herbs Work?'.

Sumac-ade is not strictly a tasty beverage, but I dare say it's the most superior method for extracting sumac's healing qualities and flavours (though I've enjoyed it as a bitters). Technically, it could be termed a 'cold infusion'.

## Ingredients:

- ✧ 4-5 drupes (clusters of sumac berries)
- ✧ Cold water
- ✧ Sweetener of choice (agave nectar, honey, stevia)

**STEP 1** – Rinse drupes under cold water to remove any dirt, debris or insects. Rest assured, however, that the berries are just fine to use for infusion if you're concerned about any microbial activity (sumac is strongly anti-microbial).

**STEP 2** – Place rinsed berries into a clean dish or pot filled with room-temperature water. One sumac drupe will strongly infuse around 1 cup of water, so keep that in mind as you add your water (to guarantee stronger flavour, however, feel free to add more).

**STEP 3** – Agitating the berries and drupes will speed up the extraction and add flavour. Simply use a potato masher, large spoon or even meat tenderizer to crush the berries a bit before letting the passive extraction happen.

**STEP 4** – Let the berry extraction steep for at least a few hours or even overnight. The longer, the better.

**STEP 5** – Once satisfied with appearance and flavour, strain out the berries and twigs from your sumac-ade. You can use a fine strainer, cheesecloth or whatever you prefer – the finer the better. My favourite method is to use a French press.

**STEP 6** – Pour the strained sumac into a glass and sweeten to taste. I like to drink it cold, or over ice, to hail the transition from late summer into autumn.

# Valerian
## (*Valeriana officinalis*)

ENERGETICS
**Cool**

FLAVOUR
**Bitter, Aromatic, Slightly Sweet**

PARTS USED
**Root**

BEST PREPARATIONS
**Decoction, Poultice, Syrup, Vinegar, Shrub,
Tincture, Extract or Bitters**

PROPERTIES
**Antiseptic, Digestive Bitter, Nervine,
Sedative, Styptic**

I love valerian – and not just because the plant has helped lull me to sleep many a time. The herb has a strong connection to Celtic roots and Druidic practice that has been lost over time, and it once was esteemed (and still is among a few, I'm sure) as a ceremonial and magickal herb – and, surprisingly to some, as a wound cleaner and healer, too. It is a sedative, so much so that it could easily be called a narcotic – but it is hardly intense enough to become addictive or habit-forming, which is why it can be easily found and sourced in tea form.

Compared to other sedative herbs like hops and lemon balm, its effects are far more palpable immediately after taking it. Whereas one minute I thought I couldn't sleep, a few moments later I would find my eyelids to be heavier. My very first time taking valerian root was in a concoction of other herbs, and its effects surprised me. I didn't believe that something botanical and natural could knock me out so quickly. I woke up, a little embarrassed, in a room that was now empty of the people that were in it before, realizing I had fallen asleep in a soft chair in the middle of a gathering. A strong testament to its effectiveness – and it hasn't failed me since. People should not underestimate its other ancient uses, for digestion and as a wound healer, though these are less potent compared to other plants, like angelica or pine. That said, it far outweighs these other categories as a sleep-supporting herb.

**Warnings before use:** When used conservatively, occasionally and as directed, valerian is a perfectly safe and effective herb for sleep. However, among some people it has been reported that valerian can have the opposite effect: giddiness, alertness and hyperactivity. Of course, if this happens to you, seek out a different sedative herb to help you, such as lemon balm or hops.

Avoid consuming high amounts of valerian root tea, extracts or even supplements, no matter how much you struggle with getting to sleep. This can cause nausea, vomiting, confusion, headaches, dizziness, giddiness and all sorts of unpleasant side effects. It's generally recommended to avoid using valerian in children, or in women who are pregnant or nursing.

## BASIC VALERIAN BITTERS RECIPE

Valerian is a tricky herb, as its flavour is unpleasant to some, whether in tea or tincture form. But this doesn't make its sleep-enhancing effects any less desirable. I recommend adding a little sweet and acidity to a bitters recipe featuring valerian (see p. 66 for more info on bitters creation) or, inversely, to flavour an already fully potent tincture.

## Ingredients:

- Valerian root (preferably fresh, though slightly dried is OK)
- Citrus zest of choice (orange, grapefruit, lemon or lime)
- Sweetener of choice (honey, agave or syrup)

**STEP 1** – Place valerian root, fully processed (chopped or ground), in a clean Mason/Kilner jar or other container that is food safe and airtight. Pour alcohol over the ingredients until they're substantially submerged.

**STEP 3** – Store the jar in a cool, dark place – only overnight if you would like subtly flavoured, low-potency valerian bitters. Or, if you want very bitter, high-potency valerian tincture, let it steep or macerate for at least a month. Give it a good shake a few times whenever you remember it.

**STEP 4** – After an overnight steep (or when a month is up), strain the bitters concoction through a fine strainer or cheesecloth into a separate clean container.

**STEP 5** – Add up to 1 tablespoon of your zest of choice to the strained tincture of bitters, as well as a sweetener to taste. Let this newly flavoured valerian concoction sit overnight, or around 12 hours.

**STEP 6** – Remove or strain out the zest. Taste test for sweetness and acidity, then add zest or sweetener until the desired balance of flavours is achieved. When done, store in a dark place, preferably in dark amber glass containers (blue or green work well too).

# Personal Constitutions & Herbal Energetics

When first studying herbalism and the specifics of each herb, the idea of having to memorize *every* single detail about the plant and what it may do can be overwhelming (and when you go about it that way, it can be a real task). Herbal properties can seem random at first – that is, until you get introduced to herbal energetics and energetic constitutions.

Herbal energetics can help key you into the overall effects of a herb at a quick glance, and even categorize different herbs together, helping you remember their specific effects simply by association. It certainly helped me (and still does), as well as many other home herbalists and practitioners. Energetics aren't always included as sections to intro herbalism books for healing, but I couldn't resist it since it has been a boundlessly helpful tool.

**As you read the monographs of different herbs in the previous section – and through the next section on Tastes of Herbs – you will notice the modifiers 'warm', 'hot', 'cold', 'cool', 'dry', 'damp' and 'moist'.** These are a nod to the classic systems of herbal energetics that we have to thank for this type of understanding, specifically Ayurvedic medicine and Traditional Chinese Medicine, which generally have more complex systems of herbal or alternative health energetics (the section in this book being only a simplified version). That's not to say there aren't other basic energetic approaches to using herbs for healing found in other cultures, including in modern Western Herbalism.

You'll also notice that energetic qualities don't just apply to the herbs…they apply to people too. Do you think you are a warm, dry person? Or maybe cool and damp? (Yes, you can be more than one – though you can't be dry and damp or hot and cold at the same time, of course.) **Taking cool herbs if you have a warm constitution, or dry herbs if you have a damp constitution, for example, is said to bring your body and health back into balance and holistic homeostasis.** Following this categorical way of thinking and determining the best remedies for yourself can be extremely helpful, especially if you don't know where to start finding the remedies that could help you, or you're uncertain of your 'allies'.

**Categorizing herbs can also be 'elemental', correlating to earth (cool/cold), fire (hot/warm), wind (dry) and water (damp).** That said, using warm/cool/damp/dry with energetics better taps into the wisdom and knowledge of most herbal energetic approaches. You may already be intuitively drawing upon the basic idea: if herbs are cool or cold, they could be beneficial to warm people or warm conditions, and vice versa. And you'd be right. The same goes for dry remedies for damp constitutions or conditions, and this forms the basis of 'energetics'. Keep in mind: this is only a guiding principle for using herbs – it's not a hard and fast rule or something to live by. Herbs (and people) simply cannot be 'over-categorized'. In many instances, you may find yourself drawn to using a herb that simply doesn't follow energetic 'rules', or that your own elemental constitution doesn't seem to apply to (such as simply looking for sleep- or dream-enhancing herbs, like valerian and mugwort). But, when you have no idea where to start, energetics can help.

**Are herbal energetic categories rigid and static? Absolutely not.** In fact, as you do more research on herbalism, you'll find that herbalists and different modalities can have varying opinions on the energetics of certain herbs – whereas the energetics of other herbs are not up for debate (aloe being damp and garlic being hot, for example). While herbal energetics are something that clinical or professional herbalists are more apt to use, I've included a basic breakdown because I firmly believe that they are helpful to anyone getting acquainted with herbs for healing – even if it's just at home while making your own preparations and formulas, or getting to know your health and self-care needs. It can also just be a fun way to explore herbalism in general.

**Disclaimer:** This section is not designed to help you diagnose issues in yourself or others, nor to prescribe natural remedies for yourself or others – especially for serious symptoms or health conditions. It is simply meant to be an educational guide to understanding herbs and the possibility of using them in self-care.

# The warm/hot constitution

## QUALITIES | HEALTH CONDITIONS

Identifying a warm or hot person is probably the easiest and most recognizable process in energetics. It's also the easiest to recognize in most of the classic warming herbs. Someone who seems 'fiery' is most likely to be a 'hot' person, but they can also be defined by tending towards inflammatory issues, a lot of energy, a higher metabolism and higher blood pressure. Everything about the hot constitutions is a bit 'over-stimulated'. But keep in mind: energetics only represent a spectrum. Someone can lean closer to having hot constitutional issues, but have cold issues too.

Hot-natured or warming herbal remedies are not what someone with a warm constitution would be after, however; remedies of a cooling nature (listed below) are what they may need. Many of these remedies have slight to moderate sedative properties, to let cooler heads prevail. They slow down metabolism, reduce over-stimulated circulation, energy, mood and more. If inflammation is an issue especially, cold remedies are just the thing, no matter what their constitutional complexion.

Remember: this description of warming/hot energetics does not limit what hot-natured herbs are fully capable of; it is just a guide.

## TRAITS OF A WARM/HOT CONSTITUTION

- ✧ Higher cold tolerance
- ✧ Gets warm or hot easily
- ✧ Prone to fevers
- ✧ Common issues with inflammation (rosacea, reddened skin etc.)
- ✧ Digestive issues (esp. diarrhoea, high acidity, overactive digestion)
- ✧ High blood pressure
- ✧ Strong complexion
- ✧ Higher metabolism
- ✧ Inflammatory pain
- ✧ High energy
- ✧ Quick to anger or annoy, hot-tempered

## Warm or Hot Health Conditions:

- ✧ Burns (sunburn, first- and second-degree burns etc.)
- ✧ Muscle fatigue from overuse
- ✧ Diabetes
- ✧ Inflammatory conditions
- ✧ Inflammation, swelling and associated pain
- ✧ Some autoimmune conditions
- ✧ Fevers
- ✧ Hyperacidity
- ✧ Allergies (with inflammation symptoms)
- ✧ Ulcers
- ✧ Heartburn
- ✧ Hyperthyroidism

## Classically Cold or Cool Herbs and Remedies (best for hot conditions and constitutions):

- ✧ Agrimony
- ✧ Aloe vera
- ✧ Comfrey
- ✧ Cucumber
- ✧ Gentian
- ✧ Hibiscus
- ✧ Hops
- ✧ Nopal cactus
- ✧ Lemon balm
- ✧ Mint (topical)
- ✧ Pine
- ✧ Plantain
- ✧ Sumac
- ✧ Valerian

# The cold/cool constitution

## QUALITIES | HEALTH CONDITIONS

Compared to those with heated constitutions, cold or 'cool' people may be hard to spot. Their issues can be related to a *lack* of immune response or circulation, which often manifest as low energy, sensitivity to cold and issues with pain and sluggish bodily processes. Emotionally, the cool constitution is generally more level-headed – maybe too level-headed, to the point of avoiding emotion, where it manifests as physical pain and issues instead. Instead of inflammatory pain, like in the warm constitution, cold people may struggle with things like cramping, fatigue and numbness in tissues.

The warming remedies below may be perfect for these people, helping jump-start a slow immune system or circulation issues. They help accomplish what comes naturally to people with a hot complexion: they warm the body, stimulate blood flow, bring on a fever or heat, improve circulation, increase metabolism, ramp up digestion and bring a strong spike in immune response, especially if an inflammatory immune response is needed. This is perfect for colder or cooler people.

## TRAITS OF A COLD/COOL CONSTITUTION
- Lower cold tolerance
- Gets cold easily
- Slow or sluggish digestion
- Poor circulation and numbness issues
- Low blood pressure
- Pale complexion
- Digestive issues (esp. constipation, slow digestion, cramping, etc.)
- Lower metabolism
- Cramping pain
- Low energy

## Cold or Cool Health Conditions:

✧ Muscle fatigue and pain from lack of use

✧ Cramping (from lack of circulation)

✧ Arthritis

✧ Joint pain

✧ Infection or sepsis (STAPH, MERCA etc.)

✧ Cold extremities

✧ Hypothyroidism

## Classically Warm or Hot Herbs and Remedies (best for cold conditions and constitutions):

✧ Angelica

✧ Arnica

✧ Cinnamon

✧ Cloves

✧ Citrus (zest)

✧ Elecampane

✧ Garlic

✧ Ginger

✧ Ginseng

✧ Horseradish

✧ Hot peppers (cayenne, habanero etc.)

✧ Mustard (seed)

# The dry constitution

## QUALITIES | HEALTH CONDITIONS

People with dry (also called airy or 'windy') constitutions are characterized by tension, dryness, anxiety and an overall lack of health and vitality. Tissues are tight and tense, and their minds tend to be too. Dryness due to allergies or respiratory issues is possible – and of course, dry skin is too. Being 'dry' has a strong correlation to the nervous system being depleted, but it can be a general wasting away of the body with weight loss, hair loss, dehydration, kidney issues and a parched appearance or complexion. You can be a warm and dry person or a cold and dry person, as the dry constitution overlaps with these temperaments. Or you may simply have a dry condition that needs damp remedies.

Dry people need damp remedies plus some warming or cooling, depending on other dimensions to their constitution. Such remedies bring much-needed moisture and nutrients to those who struggle with dryness – but they would slip right through the holes for someone with a damp constitution. (For someone who is already damp, dampening would be their bane.) Damp herbal remedies nourish the nervous system to soothe anxiety, relieve tension, moisten skin and tissues, and bring a deficient body back into balance. They also tonify the kidneys, which can be central to the dysfunction in dryness in some cases. If you have a windy or airy disposition, your body will welcome an abundance of nutrients and moisture, ideally soaking it right up.

## TRAITS OF A DRY CONSTITUTION

✧ Dry skin, eyes, tissues
✧ Easily dehydrated
✧ Difficulty sweating
✧ Very tense (muscular and nervous)
✧ Prone to anxiety
✧ Doesn't cope well with stress
✧ Spacy, cognitive issues
✧ Extreme tension but can't relax (fatigue)
✧ Weakness
✧ Thin physique or weight loss
✧ Hair loss
✧ Tends to skip meals, low appetite

## Dry Health Conditions:

✧ Anxiety disorders
✧ Migraines
✧ TMJ and bruxism
✧ Some autoimmune conditions (esp. nervous)
✧ Asthma
✧ Dry respiratory conditions (e.g. COPD)
✧ Dry skin/dermatological problems
✧ Indigestion
✧ Kidney issues
✧ Dry cough
✧ Muscle spasms and cramps
✧ Hormone deficiency
✧ Nutrient deficiencies

## Classically Damp Herbs and Remedies (best for dry conditions and constitutions):

✧ Aloe vera
✧ Burdock
✧ Cleavers
✧ Comfrey
✧ Hollyhock
✧ Lion's mane
✧ Marshmallow
✧ Plantain
✧ Shiitake

# The damp constitution

## QUALITIES | HEALTH CONDITIONS

It can be hard to put your finger on or define the true nature of a 'damp' person. While they can be characterized by an 'excess' of something, that's not always easy to pinpoint – though excess weight or obesity can be a factor (but not always). A sense of stagnancy and an 'overloaded' constitution, in need of cleansing or detoxifying, is more accurate, and may be traced to the liver or gut health. Looking at flesh, skin tone or complexion may be a better way to identify dampness: if there seems to be sagginess, a lack of tone or pallor, and a lot of water retention, there is probably some excess to be found. Think of damp constitutions as waterlogged, or sluggish.

In that case, you can bet that you're dealing with someone who is overly damp and, as such, they'll be in need of drying or tonifying remedies to get things moving and 'aired out' again. The liver is a great organ to target, as are the gut and intestines, which will be in dire need of astringency and tonifying in order to recover their balance.

Remedies of a drying nature can be incredibly powerful and restorative for damp people and conditions. They help tonify skin and cleanse tissues, detox the liver and get fluids in the body moving and expelled to remove waste and stagnation that has been hanging around too long. Many of them are great at kick-starting the liver to get it into gear to help damp issues too.

## TRAITS OF A DAMP CONSTITUTION:

- ✧ Weepy skin, eyes, tissues
- ✧ Sweats easily
- ✧ Prone to weight gain
- ✧ Prone to inactivity/lack of exercise
- ✧ More phlegm and mucus
- ✧ Sad or stagnant emotionally (depression possible)
- ✧ Saggy or doughy complexion
- ✧ Clammy skin
- ✧ Low energy, lethargic
- ✧ May have higher appetite

## Damp Health Conditions:

- ✧ Depression
- ✧ Damp respiratory conditions
- ✧ Liver issues
- ✧ Edema (water retention)
- ✧ Overactive bladder
- ✧ Wet cough
- ✧ Lymphatic congestion
- ✧ Low immunity
- ✧ Chronic diarrhoea
- ✧ Hormone excess
- ✧ Leaky gut and Crohn's disease

## Classically Dry Herbs and Remedies (best for damp conditions and constitutions):

- ✧ Cranberry
- ✧ Dandelion
- ✧ Stinging Nettle
- ✧ Parsley
- ✧ Sumac
- ✧ Usnea

# The Tastes of Herbs

This next section is one of my favourite realms to explore with herbalism, and has informed me on a lot of my craft. Newcomers may be put off by the idea that some herbs just don't taste good – and that can be true – but whatever the flavour, it shouldn't be a mystery to new herbalists that, in many cases, flavour has a lot to do with a patron herb's healing properties (and on that note, some herbs really do taste wonderful).

Below is a guide to the different tastes you can experience while caring for the self with herbs. **Herbs are not just bitter.** If you've been fortunate enough to explore a few already, then you've no doubt also encountered herbs that are aromatic, salty or even sour – but they don't stop there. Many of these flavours have significance, and can correlate to the different 'energetics' of herbs, which you can explore in the energetics chapter.

Each flavour section will contain an extensive list of healing herbs that fall under that flavour category; there may be more than one opinion about the true flavour nature of a herb, or it may fall under more than one category. For deeper insights into the healing benefits of certain herbs, be sure to explore the monographs. (Note that strictly topical herbs, like arnica or comfrey, obviously do not have a flavour profile associated with their healing benefits, and you won't find them here.)

# Bitter

Most herbs you taste will be bitter – and that's not a bad thing. The majority of herbs have bitter properties even if they have another characteristic flavour profile that is more noticeable. Though it may be many people's least favourite flavour, bitterness is arguably the most healing of all the taste sensations, and for many reasons. For one, research shows that the bitter flavour (typically caused by naturally occurring alkaloids) has an immediate effect on the body, causing a chain reaction of physiological responses that are beneficial to you – though in excessive amounts, they can be less good for you. In fact, the body's response to the bitter flavour is theorized to be a response to possible poisons (since most plant poisons are bitter alkaloids).

- ✧ Aloe vera
- ✧ Artichoke
- ✧ Burdock
- ✧ Citrus (peel)
- ✧ Cucumber
- ✧ Dandelion
- ✧ Elecampane
- ✧ Gentian
- ✧ Hops
- ✧ Milk thistle
- ✧ Mugwort
- ✧ Valerian

Thankfully, most bitter foods and herbs (when used correctly) are far from poisonous – quite the opposite! Bitter alkaloid constituents in plants kick-start the digestive system to work harder, which amps up digestive function. Here you have the underlying mechanism behind the before (or after) dinner mint, aperitif or digestif: just the right amount of bitter helps keep things moving and digesting. It also helps regulate blood sugars, keeping them from peaking or dropping precipitously. This is an amazing ally for diabetics and pre-diabetics, or to curb the effects of too many sweets.

Gently tricking the body into thinking it's been poisoned can be an impressive catalyst for healing. And it's not as terrible as it sounds. This effect happens every time you eat healthy leafy greens, roasted asparagus, orange zest or even drink a cup of coffee. Some bitter compounds are called terpenes, and these can have stimulating (or soothing) effects on the nervous system, as in the case of mugwort, valerian and hops – and all are mildly sedative. In terms of energetics (refer to the energetics section), the bitter flavour generally has a drying effect.

# Sweet

Can sweetness be healing? If you're eating lots of sugar, no. Still, certain herbs have a distinctly sweet flavour upon first taste, and they have unique qualities too. When we bite into something sweet, the appetite is stimulated immediately. Digestion slows, and blood sugar spikes (for a small rush of energy – though this is much less the case with non-sugar sweetness). Generally speaking, more food is eaten while metabolism slows down. This can have its benefits – namely, if your body is hungry for a sudden energy burst to keep it going. Sweetness detected in most herbal remedies, however, is thanks to phytochemicals called polysaccharides that help respiratory function, immunity and more. These may not be as distinct as sugary sweetness, but they are sweet nonetheless, and hit the same receptors. What's most notable about the sweet flavour is its ability to 'moisten' and encourage the body to produce more mucus. People with dry constitutions, and with especially dry airways or respiratory issues, benefit from these classic sweet herbs, and many of them have marginal benefits too (such as boosting immunity and digestive function).

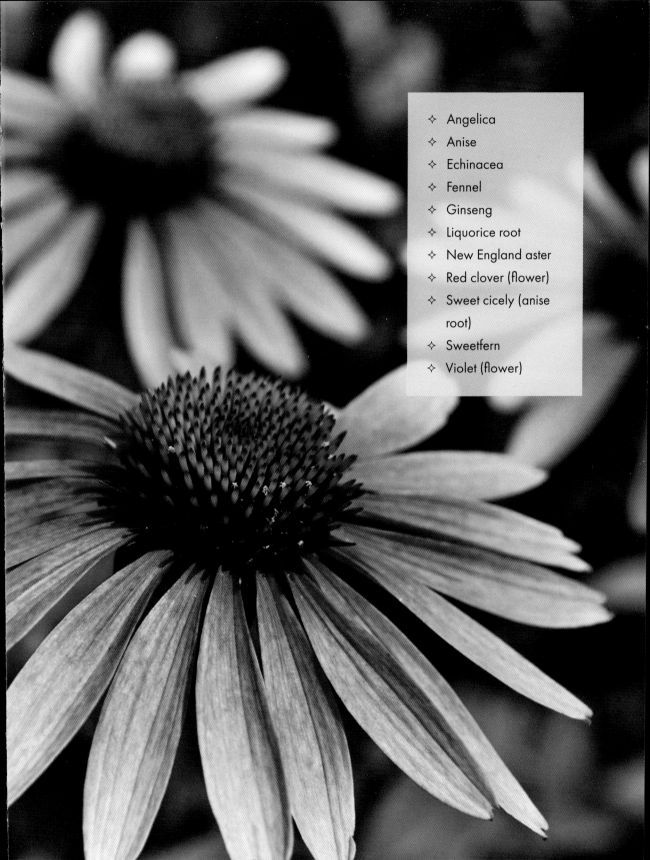

- ✧ Angelica
- ✧ Anise
- ✧ Echinacea
- ✧ Fennel
- ✧ Ginseng
- ✧ Liquorice root
- ✧ New England aster
- ✧ Red clover (flower)
- ✧ Sweet cicely (anise root)
- ✧ Sweetfern
- ✧ Violet (flower)

- ❖ Brassica/Cruciferous vegetables
- ❖ Chickweed
- ❖ Cleavers
- ❖ Hollyhock
- ❖ Horsetail
- ❖ Marshmallow
- ❖ Nasturtium
- ❖ Oats
- ❖ Sea vegetables, weeds, kelp
- ❖ Stinging Nettle
- ❖ Watercress

# Salty

The purpose of some herbal tastes isn't to boost digestive, respiratory or any other specific function. Sure, they may be able to address some of these things. But in the long run, they help everything holistically. That said, some herbs have an easy job, acting pretty much like a vitamin supplement or tonic. In short, they're purely nutritive.

When it comes to flavour, one of the quickest ways to recognize the nutritive quality of a herb is through the function of salty taste. It's a sure sign that there are minerals present, including iron, magnesium, sodium, zinc and more – important nutrients. The salt taste function accomplishes the opposite of bitter: it signals that this is a rich, tasty, nutritive food that will be good for you when there isn't too much of it (when too salty, the taste buds will be overwhelmed and reject it). The right amount of salty increases appetite and encourages you to eat more while helping the body modulate electrolyte levels and hydration, which are important for healthy lymphatic and immune function.

We all know that salting food helps enhance the flavours of meals too. That's because of the salt function's appetite-encouraging effects. Most of the herbs below have a preponderance of saltiness, but include some bitterness as well. The result: rich nutrition that is quickly assimilated by a bitters-optimized digestive system. Most herbalists agree that salty herbs tend to have a cooling effect. They can be either moistening or drying too, depending on the herb.

# Sour

Pucker up! Sour-tasting remedies have an important role in the herbal world too. Much like bitterness, sour function helps us detect acids from rotting foods that could harm us. It can also be a great indicator of important nutrients – namely vitamin C and other antioxidants. The way our bodies react physiologically to sour herbs can have even more perks, such as preventing infection or pathogens, tightening tissues, and drying up excess fluids in the body. Like the salty taste function, sour helps hydrate and balance electrolytes. It boosts saliva flow for enhancing digestion while also promoting sweating.

Topically, sour can have astringent effects that are fantastic for skin, and this astringency can also help enhance anti-microbial or antiseptic effects, making them excellent herbs for topical wound care or oral care. Across the board, herbalists agree that the sour flavour is drying and cooling. Overall, sour herbs may have the most utilitarian healing functions of all: protecting against infection, fighting pathogens, promoting fever, cooling the body, and nourishing and tonifying the digestive system, tissues and skin.

- ✧ Agrimony
- ✧ Blackberry
- ✧ Citrus (juice)
- ✧ Crampbark
- ✧ Cranberry
- ✧ Elderberry
- ✧ Hibiscus
- ✧ Nopal cactus
- ✧ Peach
- ✧ Raspberry
- ✧ Rhubarb
- ✧ Rosehips
- ✧ Sumac
- ✧ Usnea

# Aromatic

Also not an official flavour profile, aromatics are nevertheless important taste sensations – and fragrances – for healing. All the most popular selections for essential oils are aromatic herbs. You can identify them by their distinct flavours and aromas, hence their name. They can either be cooling or warming, but are almost always drying.

These herbs' powerful imprints on the senses (often making them a favourite for culinary arts or aromatherapy) are thanks to compounds called 'volatile oils'. A common hallmark of volatile oils is strong anti-microbial action, meaning the herb helps kill bacteria, fungi, and even viruses. It may also have some other specialized action: vasodilation, sedative action, anti-spasmodic (soothing cramps and muscle contractions), immune-boosting, and more.

- ✧ Bee Balm (Monarda, Wild Bergamot)
- ✧ Catnip
- ✧ Cedar
- ✧ Cinnamon
- ✧ Kava Kava
- ✧ Lavender
- ✧ Lemon balm
- ✧ Lemon verbena
- ✧ Mint
- ✧ Oregano
- ✧ Parsley
- ✧ Pine
- ✧ Rosemary
- ✧ Sage
- ✧ Thyme

# Spicy/pungent

While not an official 'taste' per se, spicy and pungent herbs are a force to be reckoned with. They have one strong affinity over all: and that is with the heart, blood and entire cardiovascular system. Undeniably warming, spicy or pungent herbs (sometimes called 'acrid' herbs) can be either damp or dry in nature but lean on the drier side of things. Their greatest ability is to bring blood flow to the skin and stimulate it throughout the body, enhancing what is called 'vasodilation'. These effects can have benefits to the respiratory system and help open up airways to ease breathing during coughs, colds, flus and other upper respiratory issues. They're also known to give a substantial immune boost to the body.

- ✧ Garlic
- ✧ Ginger
- ✧ Horseradish
- ✧ Hot peppers (cayenne, habanero, etc.)
- ✧ Leek
- ✧ Mustard (seed and spicy greens)
- ✧ Onion
- ✧ Shallot

# Savoury/umami

Salty herbs are mineral rich, while sour could mean
a treasure trove of hidden antioxidants and vitamins.
Savoury, or 'umami' remedies – which don't tend
to be classic herbs – are high in healthy fats, oils,
proteins or other natural compounds that are fantastic
targets for the brain and nervous system; lion's mane,
shiitake and other medicinal gourmet mushrooms
are the stars of the show here. Savoury remedies are
generally inflammation-fighting, immune-boosting and
nourishing as well as being nerve tonics or 'nootropic'
(mushrooms specifically). They are also cooling and
moistening, as a rule.

✧ Nuts (especially
   avocado, walnut,
   chestnut etc.)
✧ Lion's mane
✧ Maitake
✧ Puffball mushroom
✧ Shiitake